Lighten Up, You're Eternal

The Art of Deliberate Creation

Robin Richardson

Editor: Lee Parpart
Cover design: Citadel Collective
Photographer: Alejandro Collados-Núñez

ISBN 978-1-988387-24-6 (paperback)
ISBN 978-1-988387-25-3 (ebook)

This is an original print edition of *Lighten Up, You're Eternal.*

Life on Earth is a playground of creation. We are eternal beings who choose to incarnate into this dreamlike existence in order to experience ourselves. We create according to universal laws of which most of us have no awareness. We are now being urged to collectively wake up, become aware, and to begin to create our dream life by applying this new understanding and by practicing deliberate and loving creation. How does this all work and how can you know it's true? That's what this book is for. Use your discernment as you read, applying what is said here to your own experience of reality and testing it against your inner guidance and wisdom.

Table of Contents

Introduction 1

Feeling Reality 6

Meditation.. 10

Manifestation and the Quantum Field........................... 13

How Does One Align With and Know Truth? 15

Why Do We Forget Who We Are and Where We Came
From When We Incarnate on Earth?............................... 17

Communicating with Spirit/Non-Physical 25

Speak to Higher Consciousness 27

Navigation.. 32

Forming a Deliberate Relationship with Your Thoughts........ 35

The Power of Ecstasy... 37

Death.. 39

Relationships 43

Each Day 46

On Manifestation and the Law of Attraction 47

Fear 50

Elevating Feeling... 52

Affirmation 54

Affirmation for Letting Go 56

Dreams 57

Affirmation Love... 58

Mastery... 62

Affirmation Mastery.. 63

Healing 66

Affirmation for Healing 68

Boundaries and Letting Go 70

Affirmation 74

Non-Physical 75

Collective Co-Creation 78

Love 80

Meditation 83

On Stillness 85

On Children 88

Stages of a Spiritual Awakening 90

Romantic Relationships 98

Characteristics of the New Human and How You Are
Becoming It 102

Meditations and Visualizations 108

    Manifesting Abundance 108

    Manifesting Love 109

    Self-Healing 111

    Clearing Your Energy and Cutting Your Cords 112

    World Healing and Collective Elevation 114

Practices 116

    The Violet Flame 116

    Elevated Awareness 117

Triggers 121

My Story 122

Fairy Gifts 130

About the Author 135

Introduction

As a kid, I was overwhelmed by a sense that life had purpose, and that I was born for a reason. I struggled to figure out what that purpose was in a world of adults who had no answers. Over the past several years, I have, through meditation, surrender, and quite a bit of adventure, come to find the answer for myself. It is an answer that will appeal to and elevate many of you as well. It can be summed up in one simple story, taking place in all of our futures. This is the story: as we begin to slip out of the dream that is this life, into the realm of what we call death, with the rare insight that comes with letting go, we will turn around, look at all we have lived, and laughingly say, "Oh shoot, it was supposed to be fun!"

You picked up this book because some part of you knows or at least wants this to be true. You suspect that maybe life is not supposed to be just okay, and it is certainly not supposed to be a struggle.

You may have noticed lately that the things you used to think of as important no longer hold weight with you. You may have drifted somewhat from certain friends and family as your values and modes of relating changed and became more refined. There may be an increase in what seems like coincidence. The things that you think about, good or bad, come into your experience, and you have been starting to feel like life is a bit of a dream. Well, in many ways, it is. And as the world went into lockdown in 2020, many of you who were on the fence, approaching what we call divine discontent, relinquished yourselves and began to see life through fresh eyes, perceiving and feeling more spirit, more of what you would call magic. You may be familiar with the Law of Attraction — the power of thought to create reality — and you may have begun seeing proof of it in your experience.

Worldwide isolation, along with the general break in routine and profound uncertainty, has triggered a mass awakening. All you need to do is listen to your friends, tune into new music by artists you respect, and follow leading-edge scientists and thinkers to see that there are common threads of spiritual awakening sweeping the world. I won't go on about this too much as there are myriad sources on it. I will instead tell you my story by means of introducing what this book is and how to use it.

When lockdown happened, I took the opportunity to check out of my work and social life and to go within. I meditated several times a day, allowing myself to shut off all thought and worry, all notions of progress and survival. Most importantly, I shut out the voices of others I realized were so prevalent a part of the ongoing dialogue in my mind. Within weeks, tremendous shifts began to occur. I started to hear my body more deeply, cutting out coffee, meat, and processed foods of all kinds, and coming into clear awareness of the toxins in my hair care and cleaning products and their effects on my body. I could feel the state of my cells, and began to understand what they were communicating to me. My handwriting shifted, from the small, barely legible cursive it had been since I was a child, to a clear printing, easy on the hands and the eyes. I found I could heal aches and pains through my meditative states and soon realized I no longer had allergies, which had been severe, nor period cramps, which had been crippling every month for the past twenty-five years. There is so much more. As I went inside myself and became clear on who I was when not pestered with thought and duty, I became almost allergic to certain social interactions. I could see what was false, what was ego-based, and, most importantly, what was devoid of love. I was becoming myself, and myself (as you will learn through this book of yourself as well) is of pure love and is happiest when in pure love. It's really that simple.

After about a month and a half, I approached a sustained ecstasy. Everything was vivid and meaningful, and I could even feel something as simple as the fibres of my carpet with overwhelming pleasure. I could feel music all over and inside me, and most days I was brought to tears by several things that others may consider banal. At this stage I began to live in what you could call a waking dream in which everything, from the child across the street to the ad that came on before a song, was the voice of spirit nudging me ever further up this path that I had undertaken. I listened and followed these nudgings.

Here I will bring to you what they have brought to me: an accessible understanding of the underlying energetic structures of this world, giving you an idea of who you actually are and what you are actually capable of, as well as empowering you to create your personal heaven while still on earth.

Life here unfolds through forces most have no awareness of and, therefore, have no ability to control and thrive within. It is time to put an end to the blind groping and to illuminate the unseen, unquantifiable, underlying physics of your experience. Scientists cannot do this for you. Nor can you find it through worship of those that have mastered it before you. It must come directly from your relationship with yourself, through your personal experience of reality. What is proposed in the following pages is not for the faint of heart, but is for those who are restless enough, fed up enough, and bold enough to take a grand leap into the unknown.

If you are reading this, it is because you are, to some degree, open to exploring new ways of knowing and being. I ask you to let go of resistance, allow yourself to sink into the information I am offering without worrying about where the information comes from, for it makes no difference. All you need to do is read with an open mind and allow what you read to filter through your own experience and discernment. There is nothing written here that you do not already on some level know and that you have not already proved to yourself in a number of at least subconscious ways. Take what you want. Leave what you don't, and try, as best you can, to slip into this stream without resistance. There is nothing to lose in not offering resistance, and much to be gained, as you will come to understand as you read on.

Please be gentle with yourself as you read — go slowly, look up words if you have to, and take a day or two to reflect on a page or paragraph if it feels right to you. This information can be a lot to take in and it is best not to feel you have to take it all in at once. Don't try to prove anything to yourself, and don't worry if it takes a while to set in and make sense. If it were easy, we'd all be happy millionaires by now. While it may seem sophisticated, this book is meant for everyone, and I mean *everyone*. Don't let the way I write discourage you from taking everything you can from this book. It is for you and it comes to you only with the spirit of love and giving. Receive it gently and you will be happy with the gifts it yields.

Note: You will notice the use of "we" in this writing, and the referring to Robin seemingly in the second person. I wrote this book in a state of what you might call channelling, in collaboration with higher consciousness. This is not important. Most works that flow are channelled to some degree. And it is not important that you believe or accept this as you will be reading through the filter of your own discernment. I offer this explanation only as an explanation of the voice you will be hearing from.

Feeling Reality

We think by feeling. What is there to know?

— THEODORE ROETHKE

You are a timeless consciousness, fragmented out from the source of all creation. You incarnated from pure energy into physical bodies on this physical Earth and agreed to the dynamics of time, space, and, most importantly, free will in order to experience yourself more fully.

Know that being here is your choice and that you designed the trials of your life for your own benefit. Know that your essence is perfect and your wounds and distortions are exaggerated in yourself and in those around you in order to help you identify and clear them. Know that this life is created for your benefit, and know, most importantly, that it is supposed to be fun. It is the thinking mind combined with the thought forms ("ideas," "facts" and so forth) that create the illusion of suffering. If you were to stop in any given moment, even in the middle of a battlefield, and actually sink into the true energy flowing through you, you would find that all is well. It is the thinking mind that categorizes things into "good" and "bad" and thus suffers as it tries to move from the one categorization to the other. This is what the myth of the Garden of Eden is about. The truth is that Eden is right where you are standing, it always has been, and you have cut yourself out of it with "knowledge of good and evil," aka judgment. What we are offering in these pages is a road map back to this ever-present Eden, which is eager to welcome you back into its infinite ease and potential.

Awakening to this is a never-ending process, not because truth is elusive, but because reality is a co-created experience and so there is no fixed conclusion to arrive at but rather a learning of the movement of this co-created reality in order to more deliberately participate in it.

You are here to expand and refine yourself, to enjoy the tactile nature of your reality as well as the slow material manifestation and causal nature of this plane, which acts as an elaborate mirror in which you can see your inner self reflected in all that is around you. **Want to know yourself? Look at the world you are living in. Want to change the world you are living in? Change yourself.** All you come into contact with is your creation based on the Law of Attraction, and we will show you not only how to manifest based on these laws but how to liberate yourself and inch ever closer to total awareness.

Think of existence on Earth as a video game, which in many ways it really is. Your body and your mind are the avatar you have chosen. You are not them but you wear them in order to have a particular experience of this matrix. As in a well-designed video game, you master the environment through mastery of your avatar and of the ways in which the controls work and so forth. It really is the perfect analogy. And of course each time you die you may come back in a different avatar of your choosing, and you may go through new or parallel levels, now a little swifter, a little wiser, and making it a little farther along than you did the time before. This is the nature of reincarnation. This is the nature of your life and why you are here. When you get this, when you really get this, you become fearless, empowered, and most importantly, full to overflowing with love for all that you encounter because you see that it is you, your world, your heart, and your creation.

~

It is no longer enough for those who come to enlightenment to sequester themselves off in ashrams or in monasteries, tempting as it is. We wish for the masses to achieve this awareness, and we wish to teach you how to live it within a shared environment with others.

Why? Because you didn't come here just to check out. You came here to participate from an enlightened standpoint, as lucid dreamers. And because once enough of you reach this state and insist on this quality of love and life, the whole of the world and its structure will shift and no one who is enlightened will want to hide because all that is will reflect enlightenment. **You create yourself through your engagement with the world and your world is created through its engagement with you.** Therefore, accept this call, become your potential, and set the stage for those around you to awaken to themselves as well. You will see that the material result of this is profound, as shifts in your politics, education, environment, and even city planning begin to occur for the better on a mass level. You are alive at the most exciting time in the history of your Earth; you live at the cusp of the Age of Awakening — the end of all that was and the beginning of all that was meant to be. Again we will say for your enthusiastic enjoyment: return to the Garden of Eden where all is provided and all is well.

~

We want you to remember why you came here and to be excited about taking the helm of your experience and steering the world forward.

We want you to feel the never-ending love that is at the core of who you are and that is running through you always.

We want you to clear your mind and your limiting beliefs enough that you can see and experience what you would call magic and what we say is the persistent nature of your reality just below your distracted awareness. We are always loving you, and we are always communicating with you for your benefit.

Meditation

Meditation is where you make contact with the life force of all that is, with your true self, because it is where thought, with practice, gives way to presence unresisted. Meditation is the relinquishing of your relationship to the matrix in order to come into alignment with the beingness outside of time and space where truth is. It is where the illusion anchored in thought breaks down and where the higher dimensional consciousnesses may enter and communicate with you for your benefit. It is where your body begins to heal itself and your mind begins to get a whiff of the well-being flowing beneath that ever-present pest that is thought.

Begin with twenty minutes in the morning and twenty minutes in the evening. Allow yourself to sit or lie down comfortably and relax into nonmovement. Become aware of your body in infinite space and become the master of this space, monitoring each sensation and each thought with hyperawareness. Here you will learn not to engage with your thoughts. You will see how unimportant they are as you redirect your focus back always to your breath. Here you will learn to become a master of your internal environment, an energetic space which is the beginning of all manifestation, wanted and unwanted. Everything that manifests in your body and external environment begins in your energetic environment, your thoughts and feelings. This is why the practice and mastery of meditation is so important, as it is in meditation that you become the creator of all that you are becoming.

Do not worry or judge yourself as you begin meditation. Take it easy and enjoy the process. Let it be an excuse to let go and relax, like a spa break. All you have to do here is be still in mind and body and forgive yourself, swiftly returning to focus each time you are not still. The key here is focus and surrender. Focus on your breath and surrender yourself to the free fall of a thoughtless state. For you are falling, you are falling right into love and what you will find as you stay there long enough and come there often enough is what you would call miraculous.

Practice meditating for two weeks and you will notice a certain calmness and an increased awareness. Practice for a few months and you will notice physical and emotional healing as your body in rest is able to go to work on itself, repairing at a deeper level than it can when you are constantly drawing its attention up into the anxiety of undirected thought. Practice this for years and notice your entire reality change in ways you could not have dreamed up from where you are currently standing.

In meditation, the manifested ceases to be and the unmanifest potential shows itself for your sculpting. Meditation collapses space and time and returns you to your original state as spirit: formless, eternal, and unattached to the identification the personality has formed with the world. Here you know yourself through the cessation of thinking about yourself. For thought can only ever distort. We are not saying that there is anything wrong with these distortions. They are what you came for. We are saying that in order to know what lies beyond them — in order to have fun with the game, knowing it is a game — you must remove yourself from the belief that they are real. Meditation reminds you that you are in an avatar — not so that you can beat the game and get out, but so that you can relax and remember to have fun and be deliberate while playing.

Once you have touched reality through meditation, it is important to sustain it, putting it into practice in your daily life as you become an increasingly authentic manifestation of your spirit self, infusing your avatar with this truer state of being.

We will pause and say that there is a wide spectrum in what we are offering here. You can use the information to improve your life in small increments, to become more loving or to manifest with more ease, or you can take it as far as to become enlightened within this lifetime. It is entirely up to you and we trust that you will act according to the nudging of your own inner self.

Manifestation and the Quantum Field

See a complex system of webs that run within everything manifest and unmanifest (potential) on your planet. See each thought and corresponding feeling you have as firing up the energy within its own web of creation, the same way the neurons in your brain fire up when activated. The more you fuel each web with its thought and feeling equivalent, the closer it comes to material manifestation. When you combine your thoughts and feelings with will and action, manifestation becomes an inevitable result.

There are no exceptions. So, keeping this in mind as often as you can, come to recognize the impact of your thoughts and feelings — see the myriad webs around you reach out into the whole of your experience from the still point of all that is you. Choose consciously which webs you want to activate and grow and which you want to let wither and die. Let, for instance, all webs of resentment and victimhood wither by changing the story you tell others and yourself. Now fuel the webs of abundance, acceptance, and good health by appreciating and being grateful for what you can find to appreciate and be grateful for.

Maintain your energetic point of attraction in this manner, through making your life a living meditation. By this we mean to say that, by being conscious and deliberate in every waking minute, you will be able to create for yourself an increasingly extraordinary reality. You will see that nothing is random, that you are not the victim of anything, and that at your disposal at every given moment is a stream of infinite potential. We say you will see this because, as you put this into practice, you will become aware increasingly of the way in which every given day is a direct reflection of your energenic signature.

Just practice watching for it. Each time you get cut off in traffic, look inward at your point of attraction (meaning the energetic signature you carry and use to create webs). Same goes for each time you receive an unexpected smile or are approached by a child or dog. Just a few days of observation and you will see that there is no need to take our word for any of this as it is proved and evidenced in your experience in every waking moment.

How Does One Align With and Know Truth?

One lets go of one's thoughts about things and, more importantly, others' thoughts about things. One sheds societal and familial expectations — in which one compromises oneself on any level — and through romance with the pure experiencing self, comes into contact with one's own heart. There are so many cultural norms and expectations in the modern world that make this a very difficult task. Therefore, in the meantime, we do recommend as much isolation as one can manage, just to get in touch with yourself unimpeded; then you can slowly reintroduce yourself to the world once you feel grounded enough in your practice of maintaining alignment and not getting pulled into false narratives.

This process usually takes years to see through, so do not pressure yourself or rush the process. Go slow, and allow us to guide you as we inevitably will be standing by to do.

It can be a very harrowing path, finding and integrating your own truth, as you will find as you isolate and go inwards that much of who you are and what you feel is out of sync with the culture you have fit yourself into. The lower energy centres, which focus on survival and fitting in and which fuel what many call the ego, will flare up, triggered by the fear that you may be excommunicated and lose all that you have built with the world around you. This is true: you will lose what you have built — in order to make space for what you really deserve and what your heart really yearns for, which is so much more.

The task here is not to overcome the lower energy centres, so much as it is to lovingly let them know that all is well, that you know what you're doing, and that, yes, it is safe to launch off this ledge into the unknown. You will need to do this consistently, as these centres are strong and persistent. It's understandable, of course. They believe they are keeping you alive, and this is a strange tug of war with the part of yourself that is coming to know you are immortal and not at all worried about survival anymore as you set your sights on thriving. And, yes, the two are mutually exclusive. No one who is worried about surviving can thrive. It is the law.

This is easier when you scale back your perception and see the long view of your life. Will you care what your boss thinks five years from now when you are sitting on the front porch with the one you love? No. So why care now? **Let the feeling of your wonderful future life fill your present and know that anything discordant or unwanted that occurs now is a manifestation of a past you, and that you have the power to focus and create yourself into new and improved experiences in every waking moment.**

Why Do We Forget Who We Are and Where We Came From When We Incarnate on Earth?

So that you can learn and be ever refined through finding your way back to yourself on your own without knowing. This also allows for your perception of the "monsters" within you to be externalized in the seeming form of others and their actions. This way you can see them materialized and confront them thoroughly. If you knew the whole game, you wouldn't benefit from it quite as much. Finding your way back in the dark is a sure way to secure your intimate knowing of the environment. Also, you learn best when standing unarmed before the opposition of your desire and who you are. In this scenario, and only in this scenario, are you able to learn experientially that love and surrender are the only way through.

Fear drives you off the path of your best life in the form of impulsive and ill-aligned action.

Love keeps you on it with patient receptivity.

None of you are victims. All of you are the creators of your suffering and designers of your misfortunes, both as your higher self, who designed them for your own learning, and your ego self, which attracts more of them unconsciously, having not completely learned what needed learning. Understand this and you understand that, as you learn your lessons, the correlating troubles disappear. We implore you all to wake up and see the speed and accuracy in which you are manifesting — choose, therefore, to do so consciously and from a place of love and good faith.

Let life be the fairytale you know you deserve by letting go of the reasons it can't be. Life loves when you love it. Life responds to your energetic touch like a purring cat. Stroke it with thoughts of freedom and joy and it will yield to you.

~

Remember the webs of creation? Once you spin your web for joy, as a spider does her extra intricate web for catching flies, you too will begin to catch things like opportunities, confirmations, synchronicities, as well as the moods, situations, people, places, and even physical appearance and manner of the reality of joy.

See your webs filling in as you focus and as you practice the feeling of what it is you want. See the proof of it in your life as more joy comes in, making it easier and easier for you to feel it and, thus, attract it. It is the snowball effect. Once you get past the hardest part, which is the movement from sadness to joy without external circumstance giving you a reason to be joyful, then the reasons start coming and joy is not such an effort. In this way your life gets incrementally better and it becomes ever easier for you to manifest. Not to mention that as the proof presents itself, as we promise it will, your interest will turn to belief and will grow into knowing, making your manifestation power all the more potent and fast acting.

~

Be conscientious of your consumption of "information," as it is often falsified, biased, and second-hand. Each piece of information you take into your awareness and choose to believe creates its own point of attraction and begins to fill in its own web within your life. We, therefore, ask you if you're willing to design your life, based not on what seems to be most evident in the reality around you, but on what you most desire it to be. **Remember: you are not here to discover truth but to create it.** Therefore, shift your focus from what seems true to what you can make true, what you want to be true, and, more importantly, what feels good as a truth. All you need to do to understand life is to live it and to live it with a focus on your happiness as a compass. Learn to sit comfortably in paradox. Learn that it is not your job to judge, only to discern — meaning, choose wisely what you bring into your experience, but do not label it "good" or "bad" as you bring it in or let it go. It is only what you want or what you don't want.

Try to go easy on others. They are not responsible for your happiness and their actions and beliefs need have no bearing on your experience. Let them be as they are. No one owes you anything. No one needs to agree with you for you to be doing the right thing, and no one needs to be doing what you see as the right thing. Everyone is in their own learning experience, creating from the contrast they have asked for. Know this. Know that all unfolds exactly as it should, and be at peace with what others seem to you to be. This peace will free up extraordinary amounts of creative energy from your storehouse of potential, so, as you sink into acceptance of others, get excited about how much benefit you will bring into your life. At this point, the real fun is just getting started.

Replace expectation with contented enjoyment and watch how you transform those around you.

Focus on what you like and appreciate about others and watch how they take on more and more of those qualities.

~

In this new age, we see many of you coexisting in blissful independence, basking in the love and appreciation. You know you need nothing from anyone because you have mastered your webs of creation and know how to provide all material and emotional things for yourself. From this place of abundance, you may be generous with one another without fear as you realize that one's success does not denote another's failure just as one's health does not make another sick. Therefore, you will raise each other up, you will cheer each other on, and you will wish always for the best possible outcome for all in every situation. This is how you consciously create your Eden.

~

It is important to begin to distinguish the difference between the will of man and the will of spirit. How much of what you do is driven by what you perceive to be the expectations and requirements of those around you? How much of what you do is driven by the nudging of your own spirit? Is it worth the sacrifice of your spirit and your truth to deliver what you believe is expected of you? Can you take the leap and have faith that following your spirit will yield more happiness and success than bending to the will and systems of those around you ever could?

~

What else is the heaven on Earth we are guiding you towards? It is a shared space of humans who have aligned with pure consciousness and have embodied its qualities of love and expansion. It is near-instant manifestation born of real emotion, deliberate intention, and inner faith and knowing. It is delightful synchronicities and a thinning of the veil that allows you to see the dreamlike quality of this reality as well as our non-physical participation in it. It is the knowing that you are loved. It is the free and fearless loving of others unconditionally. It is easy and fun and with nothing taken for granted. It is neutrality with an appreciation for difference. It is unified harmony with nature, yielding to it as it yields to you. It is receptivity, surrender, and allowing the movement of all that is to course through you in the form of ecstasy, bliss, enthusiasm, love, and ease. It is easy communication with higher dimensional beings, and the easy integration of their wisdom.

What is wisdom? Wisdom is intuitive yielding to the most possible peace and benefit for all in every given situation, as a matter of creation or response. It does not require education or information — just that you be receptive enough to feel the flow of well-being, right action, and clear perception that is inherent in you.

One must clear one's mind of assumptions, judgments, and perceived structures of reality in order to acquire and work with a clean creative canvas. You needn't know anything — only be and surrender, at which point the flood of infinite intelligence running through you will give you all the wisdom you need in any given moment. This is what I am accessing now — not researched second-hand knowledge, but pure flow of easy wisdom, which you are free to take for your own discernment, applying and digesting what is best for you at this time.

The process of letting go is rarely, if ever, instantaneous. For most it takes years, and for a rare few, months. Even then it must be constantly maintained, like a well-looked-after garden. You do not become enlightened and then sit back free from illusion — rather you learn, moment by moment, to recalibrate back from illusion into truth and clarity, getting ever better at it as you practice. This is part of the deep value of meditation as in it you are developing a deliberate relationship with your own mind, learning to bring yourself back always to the present moment. Mastering this deliberate relationship in meditation inevitably leads to mastering this in day-to-day life. It is not that you will not be susceptible to thought or wrong action, but that you won't let it become a reality in your world, being aware enough to stop it or let it float past without engagement.

Know that your wisdom is as fluid as your reality as it is a direct correlation to your reality. Therefore, do not set rules or doctrines for yourself, but let the wisdom come fresh in each instance, building on what it gained previously but not being bound by it.

Become aware that your reality is a reflection of the consciousness you are aligned with. Think of consciousness as a planet, and your point of focus/attraction/alignment as the place you live. If your city is dense and full of distress, it is because you are dense and full of distress. Therefore, to get to a more spacious, peaceful location, both literally and figuratively, you must make yourself spacious and peaceful. Of course, some internal change can come from literally moving or making an environmental change, but if you have not made a full inner transformation that meets the level of the new environment, you will only bring more of what you are into this new place. The physical external has some effect on you but it is nothing, not a speck, compared to the effect you have on it.

~

Remind yourself daily that everything you come into contact with is a mirror. Let yourself learn from it while loving all you encounter in this mirror, for it is showing you your grace, your beauty, and, at times, the ugly masks you are ready to discard. If someone or something makes you feel bad, know that this is an opportunity to look within and find out what it is you may shift within yourself, both to shift these things out of your point of attraction, and to neutralize your reaction — for the reaction is only there as long as the thing is unresolved within you. See it like this: **as a literal mirror may show you a blemish which needs tending, so too does your external environment reflect back to you those blemishes you may want to tend to.** We say "may" because only that which perturbs you needs tending, as feeling doesn't lie. **Feeling is your compass; therefore, use no other means for discernment but how a thing feels.** We stress especially not to use intellectual evaluation to override your feelings. Need we explain this or can you simply look through your own experience to see the way this habit of overriding feeling with thought pans out in your life?

~

You experience what you believe in. Therefore, "Proof comes after Knowing — never before." If you need proof, you're toast. And this is not some religious test of faith. It is a result of the structure of the Law of Attraction. You can't attract into your experience that which you don't expect to receive. The good news, for those who like a bit of proof, is that you can look back through your life, for example, for proof of the Law of Attraction, seeing that each time you believed something would happen, and set your focus upon it, it happened. This, unfortunately, usually applies to unwanted experiences, as you tend to find it easier to believe in what you don't want than what you do. It feels scary for many to believe in and expect good things, for fear of disappointment, perhaps. We sympathize with this, but if you want a good life, you must get over this, appreciate the risk in light of the reward, and learn to let go of attachment in order to avoid disappointment.

The sweet spot for mastering the Law of Attraction is easy expectation. Negative expectation begets negative experience, begets negative expectation — see the cycle here? See how you could just as easily reverse the cycle to the positive side of the scale? (To clarify: when we say "negative" or "positive" we do not mean to pass judgement — rather to indicate that which makes you feel good and that which makes you feel bad.) Once you experience the proof of your deliberate creation in the form of manifestation, more and more manifestation will come easily. It is like anything; you gain confidence as you see the fruits of your labour, and so you approach it with increased enthusiasm and faith.

We would ask you this and we would ask you to give it real contemplation: What do you have to lose in believing wholeheartedly in something you feel you have no proof of?

Communicating with Spirit/Non-Physical

What is spirit?

Spirit is a broad title we use to refer to the myriad beings/essences/perspectives of focused consciousness that exist on dimensional fields beyond the constraints and perception of the third dimension in which humans exist in this incarnation. There is a massive spectrum of dimensionality among non-physical and so, as you ascend and begin making contact, know this and be discerning as you communicate.

Your guides and angels are loving and see so much that you don't. They will never lead you astray; however, do not put them on a pedestal. Know that you too, in essence, are non-physical and, in some cases, your soul's evolution when not physically manifest may be farther along than that of your guides. Know that your existence is collaborative. That you are all in this together, and that when you reach up and allow those with a higher vantage point to guide you, you are able to find the buried treasure your human vantage point never could have located.

Once you begin to look for and interpret spirit in the world around and within you, it takes notice and makes increasing effort to dialogue with you. It's like the Law of Attraction (LOA): the more you look and expect, the more you create. Expect that they are reaching out, expect that they love you and want your greatest good, and this is what you will receive.

There is no fixed modality or language here. Set your own modality based on what feels best for you. Create your own mythology, see angels your way, hear them your way, for they whisper to you, not from their original voice, but in the form that best responds to your emotion and expectation. So what we are saying is: focus less on learning the communicative modes of the universe and more on creating your own communicative modes, from your heart and your joy. If you feel spirit through dance, then dance, and if you understand the signs of spirit through synchronicities, songs, numbers, and so forth, than that is how spirit will communicate with you — for spirit is always eager to interpret your expectation and move into your field of view in order to guide you. At a point, you will begin to see that there is nothing that doesn't have some element of guidance in it.

As in prayer, hand over your trouble or roadblock to spirit and look for the guidance it brings. Much like the algorithm on your newsfeeds, spirit listens to what you need and want and delivers the relevant information.

I have stopped researching ailments and their cures. Instead I ask spirit for the best course of action, then wait until it comes into my awareness through conversation, an ad, meditation, and so forth. Take note of anything that pops into your awareness and know that it is a message, especially if it is not the result of intellectual progressions, but rather spontaneous.

Speak to Higher Consciousness

Prayer and intention setting must be accompanied by corresponding feeling or spirit can't understand it — words without feeling are mere abstractions, from our vantage point. The same goes for all deliberate manifestation — it is your feeling combined with your intention that sets materialization into process. You can't merely go through a series of motions and expect results. This universe is built entirely of energy and thus for anything to be pushed along into being it must be backed by the force of energy — more specifically, the energetic equal of that which you desire to create. For instance, you can't manifest a loving relationship while in a state of resentment. You can't heal yourself while feeling sick. You must find the feeling first and hold the intention of it long enough for the program to begin to take shape within the matrix.

So much of how people function presently is the other way around: one has an experience they don't want and so holds the feeling of that thing they don't want while wishing for what they do want. One must instead go inward, balance oneself out through meditation, and inhabit the feeling of what one wants before it has materialized. You can see this so evidently in your experience. Is it not the happy person at the dinner table who ends up having the best evening and is it not the miserable one who encounters bad interaction after bad interaction?

~

Remember, **words are abstractions without the corresponding emotion.**

It is easier to infuse your words with the necessary emotion when you write them down or say them slowly, deliberately, and out loud. Saying them in your mind, or even not saying them at all, will still be effective with the right amount of emotion and desire. Emotion and desire are inevitable attractors.

Always follow your heart. Do not accept orders or directives without first checking your internal guidance system (your feelings). Some things may be scary or uncomfortable, so we don't mean to have you avoid these; just check with yourself to see if it feels like a direction headed to joy, healing, and freedom or to suffering and subjugation. Your team will never lead you to the latter, but as you learn to communicate with your team, you may mistake others' guidance or misread the signs and take a wrong turn — this is why your compass of feeling and discernment is so important. Know that even missteps and wrong turns, are of value, refining your guidance system if you choose to let it, and giving you the opportunity to reevaluate your technique.

~

Why do we call it the narrow path of ascension?

First of all, we will define ascension, without getting too technical. This is your lightening up. Imagine you are weighted down to a three-dimensional Earth with the baggage of limiting beliefs and thought forms. To ascend into higher realms of consciousness, to ascend the spiral, you must become lighter, in a spiritual and mental sense. So each time you unload a layer of weighted beliefs, of attachment to the illusion, you move a little higher on this spiral. Now see this upward spiral as one that begins rather wide, and narrows towards the top. At the early rungs as you move up, you still carry with you distortions and ideas of polarity and therefore, move in a wider spiral with more diversity. Now the more you shed, the less room you need to move from one extreme of your consciousness to another. You no longer carry guilt, for instance, so the guilt experience is wiped from your spectrum. As more is wiped, your spirals become smaller and smaller, closer and closer to the truth of all that is which is so pure in beingness that swings not at all. This is what the creator is and this is why it created — it wanted to swing or, better put, it felt the overwhelming urge to become that which could swing back eventually to itself, expanding through the very diversity you are in and you are moving back through towards your source.

Imagine that as you made the decision with conviction not to get cancer, the grocery stores stopped carrying anything that contributes to cancer. Your free will is narrowed through a lessening of the options you have elevated above. It is natural and good and by no means detracts from your uniqueness. You are still the creator, you are still at the helm, you have just chosen to move past the broad spectrum of harmful options available to you in the third dimension.

~

Unconditional love must begin with the self, then radiate outward. It cannot be given by one who does not possess it. Therefore, be selfish and sequester yourself in your bliss for as long as it takes to come into this self-love. Others may believe that they benefit from your suffering, your dutifulness, your sacrifice, but it is not so. They benefit from your joyful and loving presence. Therefore, be bold enough to take this step, in spite of how it may appear to others, knowing that their perception (your perception of their perception) should never be taken into account when considering the courses of action in your life.

When you are not in a state of love, you are not in a state of truth — you are discordant and, therefore, the words, actions and vibrations you offer others will be discordant and harmful as well. Know this: just as the world reflects you to you, so too do you inflict upon the world what is inside you. You cannot do actual good, no matter how materially good it seems, if you are acting from a distorted, unloving vibration. Even a meal you cook out when you are out of alignment carries into those who eat it the effects of that vibration. Because all is vibration. Remember the material is the manifestation of the vibrational resonance. Be aware, therefore, both of what state you are in when you produce, and what state others are in when they produce something or communicate something. Again, use your feeling, not your logical investigation. Someone can have a reputation of being joyful and enlightened, but if they make you feel bad, you are in the wrong place at the wrong time.

All of this helps illustrate the difference between discernment and judgment. **Discernment is the use of your feeling compass to move towards or away from something — to judge it would be to carry it with you in your mind, being affected by the feeling instead of using the feeling to steer you where you need to go.** This is so, so, so, *so* common a misstep with humans. You feel a negative emotion and then ruminate on it and what caused it, when what the emotion is there for is to guide you so that you no longer need to feel it. This is how physical pain works, and you have a grip on that — pain indicates something needs to be fixed. Act on the pain when it arises and you eradicate it — ignore or sit around complaining about it and it grows stronger. Pain and negative emotion are the exact same function — they tell you something is wrong. They are not there to torture you, they are there to get your attention so that you identify and rectify their cause. Then you can move back into your natural good-feeling state and enjoy your search for more things that support that good-feeling state.

Navigation

You do not owe your fellow humans labour in exchange for a fruitful existence. This is a man-made fallacy which keeps you exhausted and divorced from your true self and your true abundance potential. In order to know this, you must return to what you were as a child and go forth with the pure potentiality and honesty that existed there before other humans began to explain their version of reality as though it were the only option.

There is a spectrum here, of course, from large scale agreed upon seeming realities such as the stock exchange, and there are more familial and personal ones such as financial struggle or wealth-mindedness. You fall somewhere on both spectrums depending on your spheres of influence. It is not important to identify and analyze them — this is a supreme waste of energy. You need only to let them go and begin fresh, moving forward through your own experiential perception, desire, and faith that what you see and desire, you will make your reality.

Getting what you want begins with saying no to what you don't want. This may seem simple, but look at your life and ask yourself how many moments were spent in compromise of your desire and your truth for the sake of others or as a result of some ideal or identity you have set for yourself. Maybe you have ideas about where you should be in your life and what you should be doing. Maybe you have ideas about the kind of partner you should have or the way you should speak to your mother — each carried idea about yourself as you live it removes you from fully inhabiting your authentic self, which defies definition and acts not on "shoulds" but on joyful "wants." See further that the only way to halt your progress towards your desired manifestation, your wonderful heaven on Earth life, is to stop along the path and settle into anything that is less than it. Visit, sure, sit in the homes of all those on the path to your castle, learn about them, learn from them, explore and have fun with them, all the while knowing they are stepping stones, they are not the destination. Visit with but do not marry until your heart sings out, "This is it! This is my castle!" Even then, of course, you are nowhere near the end because you are eternal and are eternally expanding. There is no end.

Please do not let yourself fall into the trap of believing that less than your desire is right for you. Do not on any level believe that you are an exception to this law or are incapable of seeing it through. You are divine and worthy beyond words, and all the forces around and through you are tirelessly committed to seeing you through to your best possible manifestations. ("Best possible" being qualified by the level of good feeling they bring you.) So let them help you move ever upwards in your feelings and perception, and let them guide you to your next buried treasure by strictly limiting how distracted you become on the way there. The more quickly you move through your lessons and the briefer your visits (meaning you move on when they have served their purpose), the more rapidly you ascend and live your deliberately created dream.

~

Another gateway to settling is fear and loneliness. You may sidetrack or even backtrack when you feel the isolation of your own progress and, therefore, be tempted to move back into the known, which is by its very nature, inferior to the unknown as the unknown is what lies ahead in the path of ascension and the known, behind. Fear again is your greatest captor as it motivates you to pull back instead of forging ahead and, therefore, stops your progress in its tracks. Therefor watch what is motivated by fear and what by love and always follow love.

Forming a Deliberate Relationship with Your Thoughts

To master your energy and thus your life, you must learn to see and manage your thoughts as closely and with as much care as a director watches a scene they are creating in a film. See their implications, their effect, their nature, their usefulness or uselessness and, as discussed, do not judge them but discern, becoming deliberate in what you think in order to create your ideal point of attraction. Again, meditation is the key to mastering this — as is keeping a diary in which at the close of each day you ask yourself what you gave focus to and how it served or failed to serve you. Note also where you felt you were in alignment and where you were out of it. Note how the situations in which you were out of alignment played out and do the same for the ones where you were in alignment.

Do not react to your environment, situation, interactions, and so forth, but rather receive the lessons in them and see them as an opportunity to refine the your wisdom. Each person you interact with is a character in your video game, and as you learn to navigate them with increasing skill, you move up in levels. This goes for all of your progress — things get bigger, better, and more challenging to match your expanding skill set. Eventually you barely notice the challenge because you are an intuitive master. You are in flow. From this point you begin to set the tone in a room rather than succumbing to the tone that was there when you arrived. You do not get bummed out by a party of bummed out people, but rather you enliven a party of bummed out people by the sheer presence and power of your elevated state.

The Power of Ecstasy

Waking up to your true nature happens most easily through states of ecstasy because it is in ecstasy that you abandon all that you think and all that you think you are. It is here that you surrender to the flow of pure beingness and allow all that is to flow through and move you.

We refer not to the orgasm, but to the inhabiting of pure love in every cell of your body — the ecstatic inspiration and pure feeling of exhilaration. Ecstasy draws you up the spiral of your own energy centres — opening the flow of the heart so that your life force may run up through to your throat, third eye, and crown. This is when you really open up your awareness and begin to see the dream nature of life. It may come through art, dance, lovemaking, meditation, silent sitting, or music. It may come for as little as a moment or last for hours. Its healing powers on your body and emotional mind are profound — like a blast of perfect wellness inserting its potential on the whole of your being waving, "Here I am. Here is what I feel like, and here is the blueprint to build me within yourself." Your cells now have this blueprint and begin to work towards it, knowing that they always move in the direction of your point of attraction. Once you make ecstasy the standard or at least the goal, you tell your whole being to step its game up and it listens. Ecstasy also elevates brain waves into a gamma state which is where genius level creation and problem solving occurs. When you sustain this state repeatedly, you elevate yourself to what you would call super human in your healing abilities and what we would call your natural though unexplored birthright: all of you.

~

See Earth for the school it is: a school in which you define your own lessons, adhering to the laws of karma and attraction, and in which you are meant to have fun with the spectrum of duality available for you to explore a wide range of experience. In the higher dimensional realms, as we described the narrowing of your ascension spiral as you move up to truth, there is very little sway in our range of experience and feeling. It is true that it is easier and less painful, and it is true that it is where you come from and where you will return. But see then that you came here to the broad spectrum of duality, choice, and free will in order to play in and learn from more variety than you ever could in the realms of love and higher consciousness. It is in your very forgetting of who and what you are that you are able to fall into the diversity necessary to learn at such a deep level.

Your inner being loves this opportunity so much. It loves knowing that it is evolving through every negative experience you have because you learn, whether you know it or not, always, on some level. You can't help but learn and you can't help but expand.

Death

Understand that death is by design — it is the end of a cycle of physical incarnation and the return to spirit in order to evaluate and design the next experience in your evolution. Understand that the means of death is contracted and designed by you. It serves your highest good, either as reset when all has gone awry and it is unlikely to make progress in this lifetime (this is most commonly what's happening when people overdose or drink themselves to death), or as a perfect point of departure based on achieved evolution and the lessons needed from the means of death before beginning the next cycle. Some that choose to go very early, small children and so forth, often choose to go when they do because they feel in over their heads, so to speak, and sort of hit eject on the whole experience. This is no reflection on them or on those that birthed them — it just means they choose to re-evaluate their design and come in through a different entry point with a bit more preparation. For some it will mean not coming back at all, but the availability of this option depends on the level of evolution.

Another consideration from the vantage point of one faced with the death of a loved one is to see that in their non-physical form they are able to see you and be there for you on a level of purity their physically focused self never could. In this way, appreciate the intention behind death as well as the advantage of it. Know that all that is lost is a physical manifestation full of human baggage. What is gained is the presence of the pure beingness of the one who passed. Know also (and this you can verify by asking most who have died and been revived) that the ecstasy and ease and relief of dying is most wonderful — the most wonderful, and that, as you all are moping around feeling bad about what happened, the one who has "died" is likely laughing at you and certainly wishing you would cheer up about the whole thing.

Knowing this, bring joy to a funeral — bring colours and celebration of a life and its impact. Be aware of the presence of the one who has died and send it love, show it your joy, celebrate what it was and, even more so, what it now is. Give the dying and the dead all the joy and celebration you give a newborn, for this is their most profound birth — the birth back into their non physical self, out of the limitation and distortion of their physically focused incarnation. There is literally no reason to be sitting around someone's death bed being sad — this only messes up the wondrous experience that is making this transition.

From this higher vantage point and from your spirit's vantage point, you all are popping in and out of lifetimes like whack-a-moles. It's no big deal. Even when the means of death seems painful and dramatic, know that it too was by design and the end of it is a release like you cannot imagine based on your spectrum of incarnated experience. For some of you this may strike a chord, attached as you are to placing judgment on pain and death, but consider the constructiveness of your judgement and resistance. Is pain not inevitable? Is death not inevitable? Therefore, why resist or deem bad that which you cannot change and deep down don't want to? Remember, pain teaches you and death releases you. Remember nothing and no one benefits from your feeling bad. Even if they say they do, even if they say they want your rage to match their injustice, they can only go so far as to want it. This does not make it good for them, and it particularly doesn't make it good for you. Your rage and your sadness detract from your ability to effect positive change. Rage kicks one's nervous system into survival and thus lowers the brain and body's ability to think and act clearly. So if what you want, for instance, is to effect positive change in your community, you make much more progress in your strategy and execution from a clear-headed place of calm and, better yet, compassion, than from a place of discordant rage or debilitating sadness. So give death and disaster your best, not your worst. **What needs changing does not need your reaction to change it, but your deliberate response. You can't pull another into the light if you are standing with them in the dark.**

Acceptance and appreciation of death goes hand in hand with acceptance and appreciation of the fluid and impermanent nature of your reality. Change is the necessary climate for creation because it is through change that the new comes into being. You can't create from a fixed and final point. You can feel the lack of creative motion, for instance, in your own stagnancy, and you can see that the more one is fixed in their view, the less they have the ability to learn and grow. All things are like this. To be fixed and permanent would be to petrify. Be aware of the fluidity of your experience and see yourself as the likewise fluid axis around which all else evolves and revolves, ever-changing as you inevitably ever change. See the infinite spiral of potential in this ever-growing, ever-changing relationship. You did not come to rest in easy comfort and stagnation, but to dance the often uncomfortable but ever rewarding dance of expansion with an eye ever towards the new/unknown. So see death for what it is: a necessary component of this change. See divorce this way and illness and surprise bumps in the road. See them as the instruments of change that they are and embrace them as opportunities to go into new unknowns. Know that often such jarring life events and instigators of change come about when one has stopped too long or settled in too comfortably to what was only supposed to be a lesson — a stop along the way to one's more full potential. These events are meant to shake you awake and force you back out onto the road of your life.

Learn to embrace discipline and play in equal measure. Always question the quality of your time spent and think on how you could spend it more to your benefit. We do not mean this in a capitalistic producing way, but rather we ask you to look at what brings you joy versus what comes easily — to look at what improves your quality of life versus what detracts from it. The discipline to stretch in the morning and the allowing of yourself to play with the dog for half an hour will yield you a better life by far than what results from scrolling through social media and then showing up to a job with no play. When you eliminate aimless distractions, you allow yourself the space to sink into your present experience where all potential, all love, and all higher dimensional communication lies. Distraction comes in the form of thoughts as much as from technology. It comes from anything that takes you from engagement with the now moment and all its bliss and truth and teaching.

Relationships

Imagine this: you are whole and happy and deeply content while enjoying an easy optimism about the future you know you are creating. You have a masterful relationship with your thoughts, understand your emotions as indicators rather than rewards and punishments, and you are not ruled by your circumstances but rather know that it is you who rule them. You know that what you want comes easily because you experience it continuously. You want for nothing and yet you are aware of the value of companionship and have a deep appreciation for it. This is when you have created a fertile environment for your healthy relationship. Until this point any relationship you have will always mirror that which you have not mastered and will, therefore, usually be reduced to a lesson. Now your healthy relationship will have lessons too, of course, everything does, but they will be lessons that the two of you balance and grow through rather than learning through the mistakes you make with one another. Know that all of these levels of relationship are valid — the unhealthy mirroring ones create rapid growth and prepare you for the healthy one, if you choose as with all things to take your experiences as lessons rather than punishments or proof of unworthiness. Know that any problematic or seeming negative habit or attribute you reveal in yourself is not you, it is not intrinsic to who you are. You are pure divinity. It is merely a bad habit picked up through others around you on the Earth plane which needs addressing and clearing in order to return to the clarity of who you really are. Knowing this makes accepting your lessons much easier as you won't be so inclined to take the process personally.

So here you are, clear and whole and ready. Now you are in vibrational alignment with someone else who is clear and whole and ready. You have both done your inner work, know how to navigate your thoughts and energy, and have faced and integrated your shadows in healthy ways. You are not reactive but constructive and know beyond anything the values of love, compassion, and honest communication. You are both inclined to notice and, therefore, bring out the positive in one another. You want the best for one another and celebrate the best in one another. You understand change is inevitable and so do not wish to maintain any particular state in them or in the relationship, but mutually support growth on all sides as you explore and expand, together and independently. There is nothing to hide because you know it is the whole of you they love without expectation, and you are able then to relax into your true self in every given moment. You no longer crave sweet lies, but love each other enough that hard truths are even more exhilarating. You encourage one another's passions and connections, knowing that whatever connections you make will only enhance the energy of the relationship. You are not afraid of losing one another, both because you have trust in the love and because you accept change and loss with happy wisdom. The old idea of the six-month honeymoon phase goes out the window as you commit to starting fresh in every living moment, knowing that nothing is accumulative and nothing need dwindle and die out. You know that a miracle is still a miracle even if it happens every morning and so every morning you embrace, knowing that you are embracing in celebration of the miracle of your companionship. Imagine you are never too much and never too little because you come with no expectations but rather acceptance of you exactly as you are in every fluctuating moment. Imagine flow without resistance. Communication without hesitation. Intimacy without fear. You feel inspired and motivated to try new things because you know they are as thrilled by your exploration and expansion as you are by theirs. You are so secure in your love and so grounded that the future is never a concern, nor is the past. The now is too good, too rich and wonderful to waste a moment of it on contemplation of anything outside of it and so through this love you increase your capacity for presence, for communion with the divine which can only exist in the present. You know you have made the right choice and so have no split energy, making you a stronger magnetic force within the Law of Attraction. Good things manifest more quickly and the world around you shifts to meet your new level of happiness.

Now in the act of reading that, especially if you let it carry you and your imagination away, you substantially began to fill out your own web of creation and have increased the attractive power of this relationship. For more of this impact, create your own affirmation, describing the relationship in as much emotional detail as possible, as though it already exists. Let yourself feel wonderful and hopeful and even expectant as you write, and you will be amazed at the shifts in your standards and the progress with regards to the relationship. Get yourself into alignment with it after this and we promise it is yours.

Expect this level in all relationships, not just romantic, and settle for nothing short of it. You will find yourself in a whole other level in life very quickly.

Remember, what you focus on you create more of, so a good rule of thumb in all relationships is to focus on what you like about another in order to create more of that quality or habit. If you get caught up in what you don't like, you only create more of that and end up discouraging the other in their growth.

Each Day

Think of your day in terms of potentials.

Ask in the morning to be delighted and surprised and then expect to be delighted and surprised. Be grateful and appreciative of whatever you can find to be grateful and appreciative of. Let people surprise you by taking off your shield of negative expectation and replacing it with positive expectancy.

Smile at strangers. Give compliments. Walk slowly, breathe deeply, and look closely. Take new routes, talk to new people, and listen to new music. Do something fun. Do something helpful. Do only one thing at a time and do it with your full attention.

Be aware and deliberate about your surroundings. Consider the sounds and images that make it into your experience, and steer your course towards those that most support your feeling good when you can.

Eat living foods, avoid chemicals, avoid fluoride, get sunshine, meditate, avoid aimless distraction, avoid the news, avoid gossip and any engagement that requires you to take a side or engage in judgment. Wear clothing that is comfortable, breathable, and movable. Commune with nature. Do not correct others but lead by example, and avoid debate or explaining yourself but carry yourself with the quiet contentment of one who needs prove nothing.

On Manifestation and the Law of Attraction

With the teachings of Abraham Hicks many have come to focus on the manifestation of material well-being and, while we love this and want this for you, we also wish to show you that, as you truly come into a sustained alignment with yourself, your love and well-being increases, and your desire shifts from accumulation for self, to service to others. Therefore when you reach this point, allow the Law of Attraction to work at that which you wish to achieve in service to humanity — attract vitality and compassion, attract well-being for those around you, attract healing capabilities and good health for all. Attract a vibrant and generous community and a world that is more open minded, heart-centered, and ready to learn.

~

We know we are providing you with a lot of new information and that it may feel like we are asking a lot of you, but we promise we are merely coaxing you back to your original glorious self through a suggested cleanse of all that the man-made world has inserted between you and that true being. Your authentic self is not angry at others or worried about the state of the economy. Your authentic self is harmonious, healthy, happy, and at peace with all that is and all that arises. Anything less than this is a creation of the world you live in, an illusion, and an opportunity to overcome and return with the wisdom gained in the overcoming. So many of you keep yourselves internally policed by the perceived thoughts and judgments of others. In this way you divorce from truth extends inward as you lie to yourself in order to avoid the judgment you anticipate. Think about the absurdity and destructiveness of this. We know it is rooted in a deep survival instinct as your lower energy centres have you constantly calculating what you need to do to fit in with the tribe, but we promise you can evolve past this. You can throw the tribe to the wind and discover who you really are — especially those parts of yourself that your fitting in has hidden from you — what Jung calls the Shadow Self. These aspects are so neglected that, without your attendance, they have grown in unconscious ways and have a life of their own you scarcely know about but always feel the results of. Think of negative relationship cycles and always feeling taken advantage of, for instance. This repeats itself because there is some untended shadow aspect at play here, the need to be loved and accepted leading to the repression of boundaries. You give more than you want to because you fear the other will leave if you give less. Your boundaries become your shadow and the repression of these boundaries leads to repeatedly being taken advantage of. Think of the repeated cycles in your life and identify their root cause — there you will find the shadow aspect that needs tending.

We are standing at the gates of Eden watching you wait around the outside saying, "We want to come in, but we are afraid so and so will reject us if we get totally honest." We are wishing you knew what was in here, how infinitely more rewarding, secure, and delightful being in the Eden of your true self is to being what we see as a captive in the illusion of acceptance offered by those who place conditions on their acceptance and love.

Be sovereign. Be willing to stand alone in all that you are without explaining it and accept that all that you are changes moment to moment. Therefore, do not define yourself but be. Be the perceiver. Be the experiencer. Be the creator. Every time you stand to pretend you are otherwise, you cut yourself off from truth and dilute the potentiality of your existence.

You cannot bring an attitude of servitude and victimhood to a place made of the frequency of truth and empowerment.

When you feel anxious and find yourself moving from one thing to the next never quite contented, it is because you are disconnected from truth/spirit. Stop and breathe and listen until you feel the stirring again, until you remember your blessings in the present moment again well enough to slip into delight and appreciating, and engagement with what is. Here is bliss. Here is potential. Here is physical and mental healing.

Know that you are enough, that this moment is enough, that whatever is right in front of you is enough because there is no distinction — all is the same and of the same source (just wearing different masks for the sake of this existence/ production of life on earth). Know that you are capable of receiving all that you deserve and desire. Know that once you learn through experience, you cannot forget, you cannot go back, not fully.

Fear

Allow your good feeling without drawing in the fear of losing it. Fear of losing what you have is the beginning of the loss because fear takes you out of the experience and, thus, begins to extinguish it. Therefore, know that fear itself is the problem, not what fear anticipates. Wipe out fear and you wipe out all it wanted to make you afraid of.

See it this way, as you sit with your pet on the porch and watch the breeze through the trees: there is no bank account, no dispute with a family member, no failed task at work. It is only the mind with its fear that can introduce these things to the experience and thus ruin the positive momentum of it. It is natural and normal for this to occur as the ego mind believes it is its job to always look out for potential dangers, identify them, and clang them around until it gets your attention. This has been exacerbated by the influences of media on the human mind as well as by the influence of those round you who, from as early as when you could first understand language, used this kind of ego fearfulness to teach you what they believed was going to keep you safe in this world.

It is time now to accept that this fearful ego tendency is not serving a purpose, and let it go with love and gratitude, thanking it for caring so much about your well-being. Like a well-meaning but smothering mother, it is time for it to back off and let you have your fun. The moment you begin to consciously practice letting go of this tendency to think and to fear, you begin to allow the pleasurable moments in your life to extend and thus snowball with their energetic point of attraction into more positive experiences. Soon you can scarcely remember what it was you feared because your experience has shown you repeatedly that the progression from where you are is always a forward one, always a positive one. And the few times there seems to be a bump in the road or even a storm, you have the wisdom to see that that too is a part of the positive progression as it helps teach, expand, and contrast so that you are better equipped moving forward to manage and appreciate the next level of goodness you manifest within your experience.

Speaking to fear again, remember that this is not a random or sporadic universe. Nothing happens by accident and nothing happens that is not in some way for your greatest good, though you may struggle sometimes to see the good in perceived tragedies. Therefore, know that you cannot encounter that which isn't meant for you. You cannot end your happiness except by your own sabotage through fear. See the paradox here? See the illusion that fear creates and how it becomes a reality where no misfortune could manifest without it?

Elevating Feeling

If feeling good doesn't come easily to you, take baby steps. Move yourself from depression to contentment by making a small adjustment in your environment. Sit upright if you have been lying down, take a deep breath without expectation, and focus your sight on something you like, maybe a plant or a picture on the wall. In this way you have allowed yourself a single step in an upwards direction on the spiral of feeling.

From here, in good time, you will be able to take the next upward step and so on. This could take minutes or it could take weeks. Time is irrelevant. Progress is all that matters, and, so long as you fix your intention always upward, always towards lightening and elevating, you can't lose. In fact, no matter what you do, you can't lose, but with upward momentum you get to experience an increasingly harmonized existence.

If you are in a riled-up state, raging or mourning, handle yourself as you would a wild stallion: Speak gently, be confident, and respect the strength and wildness of that which you are handling. Know that this process will take time. When I say "you" here, I speak about the inner being that is capable of consciously managing the thinking, feeling self as it moves through these variants. So see here your two selves — the wild stallion with its untamed but brilliant and powerful capacity to be in grace or discordance, and your inner self, which is tamer, always in the same place, harmonious, loving, and compassionate. When your stallion moves down the spiral, remember your inner being is still there holding it in perfect harmony and happy to step in as a guiding force. All you have to do is remember it, acknowledge it, and allow it to come in and work its magic through the processes mentioned above.

Your inner being is not judging you. It is not in a rush to get you anywhere. It is just happily standing by ready to step up when asked to help — the same as can be said for all seeming external forces seen and unseen in your life. You become an alchemist when you begin to shift your perspective so that what was a difficulty becomes a gift and so forth.

Affirmation

I love knowing that this life on Earth is all a sort of dream made up of very real sensations and very material and lasting manifestations. I love knowing you experience here is not all that serious. In fact, it's not serious at all. I love that when I am triggered or bothered or blocked it is not punishment or misfortune but a nudge in a better direction. I love that, now that I understand this, I can become the deliberate creator of my own experience. I love that I will not master this right away, and will never finish mastering it, but will always develop it, will always improve upon it. I love that my beautifully messy life has caused me to deepen my understanding of myself and my capacity, as well as to clarify what it is I want to create now that I am empowered to do so.

~

The most important thing about anyone and anything is how it makes you feel.

As you practice this conscious maintenance of your life through navigating feelings and watching thoughts, you become increasingly intolerant of all that falls below the increasingly high bar you set for yourself. You literally vibrate out of the vicinity of anything that does not resonate with what you are increasingly becoming. As you vibrate out of what you know, imagine yourself as being in a cocoon with the knowing that you are there to become a butterfly, or, likewise, a seed in the dark of the underground who knows it is on its way to becoming a tree or a flower.

Know that you are not perfect, needn't be, and never can be, because all is in flux and all is expanding. Perfection is the still point from which all this arose. It was where the creator was when it became interested in being anything but its perfect thus stagnate self. You are dynamism on purpose. Embrace this as you ascend, knowing you are not to arrive anyplace in particular or check off any boxes, but merely to continue ever in the direction of that which feels good because that which feels good points in the direction always of better.

Affirmation for Letting Go

Today I let go of anything that no longer serves me. I cut all contracts and energetic cords in order to start anew from this improved and clearer vantage point using my discernment. I let go of any guilt associated with past relationships or perceived failings on my part or on the part of others. I let go of the desire for retribution and closure. I let go of the need to explain myself or to be understood by others, knowing this is a futile squandering of my energy and theirs. I release shame. I release fear of failure or attack. I know I am safe. I know all is well. I release all inherited ideas, making room for my own interpretations of reality through experience. I release fear of the new and fear of the unknown. I release resistance and doubt. I release any resistance I may have to my inner guidance as I learn to trust my feelings and my instincts. I release all thoughts of those who transgressed or hurt me. I recognize that carrying the thoughts of them only continues to hurt me and makes no impact on the situation. I let it go. I let it go. I release any ideas I have about sacrifice and martyrdom. I release lethargy, distraction, disease, and judgment. I know that with each thing I release, I lighten myself. I feel myself getting easier to be and to be around. I feel myself expanding into the empty space each of these relinquishments leaves behind, filling the space with new potential and with bright, easy, lovely vibrations and positive points of attraction.

Dreams

Pay attention to your dreams. They have so many valuable functions. Consider them as intensive existences. They face you with yourself in ever more exaggerated forms than "waking life" in order to aid in your development. Often you are overcoming limitations, facing fears, and growing yourself unconsciously each night, and the more you become aware of this during the day, the more you have to learn from it.

In dreams you are tested repeatedly until your response begins to shift and, thus, the severity of the tests subsides. In dreams you face your shadow in many forms, slowly recognizing yourself in it and overcoming the initial repression.

Here you unlock new potential as you become integrated. However, you may be stuck or struggling with a given shadow aspect or distorted habit, and however tormenting your dream life may be, remember that it is not all that serious. Have a sense of humour and a sense of wonder about it. We do.

Affirmation Love

I open my heart to humanity without limitation or reservation. I know that I am safe by the navigation of my own discernment and mastery of my point of attraction and that I can, therefore, freely open myself in love to all that comes my way. I know that all is well and that through the lens of unconditional love I will see and experience increasingly the best in all whom I encounter as well as in myself. I appreciate that fear and guardedness are something I used to believe I needed in order to feel safe, and I happily release this outdated belief in favour of the richness that comes with an unhesitant approach to love. I understand now that it is in fact this love that keeps me safe and not my fear. I see the wisdom of my body and my emotions and I see how they are tirelessly conspiring to keep me well. I enjoy the process of improving and understanding that there is no rush and no such thing as perfection nor right nor wrong — just varying degrees of well-being and well-feeling. I embrace each stage of my journey fully, knowing that where I am is the only place that matters. It is the only place that exists and is the only place I may act from. I enrich my now with appreciation and happy anticipation of that which I know I have created down the road for myself. I know I am always provided for, especially when I let go and stop struggling against the flow of my well-being, and I know that all is in perfect harmony behind any seeming chaos or discord, like the blue sky unwaveringly behind the clouds. I embrace the spaciousness of my shifting reality, slowing down within it in order to feel it more deeply for what it is, which is undefinable, infinite wonder and potential.

With each breath I am becoming a better version of myself and the potentials of my life are, therefore, expanding in correlation.

As I become conscious and deliberate with my reality, all the shadows are filling with light and the nightmares are turning to dreams. I no longer need conflict and contrast in order to refine my desires and am, therefore, free to break from the illusion of duality and welcome the underlying current of easy well-being that flows beneath the illusion, always asking us to slip back into it like a child, with the innocence of one who knows nothing of right and wrong, should and shouldn't, and yet acts always for the greatest good, not by calculation, but because it is its nature.

Fall in love with yourself. Take it easy. Enjoy. Frolic. Don't be afraid to look silly or out of your mind. Watch for and enjoy synchronicities which are tripwires for your increased excitement on the way to manifestation.

Consider the impact your mood has on your family, your community, your city or town. Consider the ripple effect of a single pebble caught in cement as it is laid, or a single slanted brick at the bottom of a brick wall. Your vibration has an effect you cannot even begin to grasp and so take it and its impact seriously — you are not alone in your mood.

You are not alone in anything. Once you begin to recognize the awesomeness of this responsibility, you will understand the importance of mastering your thoughts and feelings.

Now imagine just the slightest upliftment in your community. Imagine the hearts of all those you encounter thawing a little as you pass them with your smile and your candid welcoming. Imagine the relief, the happiness, and the surprise. Let this be your inspiration upon waking, the idea of the ripple you will have now that you are intentional about what you put into your day and your community. Become the joy of this impact, and if nothing else goes right or feels worth celebrating, you will always have this one thing: you will always have your singular power to transform another's being. A smile carries as much transformative power as a bomb and this statement is in no way hyperbolic. A genuine smile in particular is so rare and so jarring that it literally shatters the walls around so many seeming obstacles in your life and in the lives of others. It turns points of attraction from meek and sluggish to rocket fast. It is your key to an easy day, easy life, easy career, and easy love. It is your greatest asset and the greatest gift you can offer another, especially when combined with its inevitable partner, compassion.

Be intentional about how you interpret the world. Know that everything is a reflection of you and yet nothing is personal. Therefore, choose the lessons without the sting of insult. Choose the challenge of finding reasons to love someone over the easy out of resentment or dismissal. Choose to discern rather than judge. Choose to breathe deeply and return ever to the moment. Choose to let thoughts give way to observation and observation result in loving appreciation. Choose to believe in miracles and to expect your manifestations. Choose to take risks that call to your heart and replace fear with a sense of adventure, knowing that you are eternal and that you came here more than anything for the richness of experience it would provide.

You are a being of infinite potential. You came into materiality through the sheer force of your creative will. You built and negotiated every facet of your life from that same will and creative power, along with the wisdom of your higher self, for the purpose of your greatest good and the greatest good for all. Knowing that all you experience is a result of your creating either intentionally or unintentionally, know that to resent what you encounter in another is to resent yourself and your creation. Instead, reassess and refine your creative direction based on what you do not like. Do not hold that other responsible for, as we say repeatedly, what you see in them is only ever a reflection of yourself.

Mastery

For many, the key and most difficult component here is faith, or even better, knowing. Creation is based on knowing and believing in that which you intend to create. It's like telling a dog to sit. It simply won't sit if you do not have genuine conviction and authority in your voice when you give the command. So too is this the way with commanding the ingredients of the universe. Feeling and conviction over words and actions. Always.

Get into the flow of what makes you happy and feel the confidence that comes with losing yourself to your own enjoyment. There is no neediness in this state, no grasping or insecurity. There is only being, and from here you have all the power in the world because you offer no resistance. Think about this in terms of taking on a task or craft. If you wish to become a master composer, you simply cannot achieve any kind of mastery if you approach your craft with divided and hesitant energy, and, more importantly, you cannot become a master composer if you set out expecting to become a medium good composer. Your expectation sets up the trajectory of your future and you cannot exceed your own expectations, at least not by much. Therefore, expect the best. Strive for the best, and know that you are beyond worthy and capable of achieving anything that brings out your passion and has you in the coveted flow state.

Affirmation Mastery

I am worthy of living what I love. I am worthy of being supported through the pursuit of what I love. Whatever my peer group and family seems to think about work and how it should be done is not necessarily relevant to me as I know that many of their beliefs are rooted in hand-me-down habits. I am ready to take a step into the unknown and take a chance on what I know is the real gift I have to share with the world. I have confidence in my abilities and, moreover, I have confidence in the universe's unwavering support of my passions and all that I do with love and good intention. I do not have to shrink myself or play down my talents to make others comfortable and I know that my greatness will only inspire them, even if they may not say so. I know I wasn't born to work hours for someone else's dream and then consume someone else's creation. I know I came to enjoy myself and that even if my circumstances now seem limiting, I have the potential to get myself into a place where I can do what I love and do it well. I believe in myself because I know I manifested my own body and mind out of pure energy and that is no small feat. I don't owe anybody anything and my worth is not evidenced in my sacrifice. In fact my worth is a given and thus I need only focus on my bliss, not because I owe it to anyone or ought to, but because I want to — because I deserve to and because it will enrich the whole experience of this lifetime and the lifetimes of those around me as I do.

And I like that idea. I like the idea of being an inspiration, of raising the bar, of bringing something new and full of vital energy to the world — something built on love, not sacrifice.

~

Good feelings mean you are being who you really are and doing what you really want to be doing. When you get here, stay here, build on it, allow yourself to get happier, and to get more excited. Let one fun thing snowball into the next, and, if a thought arises that you probably should be doing something else, know that is the ego and tell it lovingly that it is not needed right now, that all is well. Put up your gone fishing sign and do not allow the concerns of modern or social life to get hold of you. Be as a child. Lose your memory of duty and need and worry and just be. Just play.

Watch out for fixed identification with that which makes you happy or unhappy. You may deeply enjoy writing for a year or ten but that does not need to limit you to being a writer. When it no longer makes you happy, allow yourself to move gracefully into the next thing that does.

You are not here to find out what or who you are but to fluidly let yourself be an expression of all that is. All that is manifests in you in various ways over the course of your lifetime and does not seek to fix you into an identity or specialty. It evolves and changes and moves you always out just beyond your comfort zone for its own expansion through you. This is the dance of life and you cut it off the moment you resist its pull because you have begun to feel safe or comfortable or identified with a given pursuit.

Take time out each day to sit quietly, breathe deeply, and think on the awesome spirit that you are. Think of your conscious decision to incarnate and the excitement you felt at being able to feel the wind on your face and taste a bar of chocolate. Know that you were as excited about the pain as you were the pleasure, and that your coming here was a brave decision, one made in the spirit of expansion and adventure. See it as one who gets on a massive roller coaster and knows they will be strapped in for a hundred years experiencing with exhilaration every fall and every climb. Be motivated by the knowledge that the spirit of you never forgets that this is a roller coaster and it never tires of it. Know that for your spirit this century or so is an instant and it is an eternity. Embrace the Fool in you, fearlessly and joyfully trotting off the edge of the road with faith and a sense of humour. That's what you did coming here. All you have to do to see evidence of the joyfulness with which you arrived is look at a child. See their bliss and wonder — that is the spirit manifest into form experiencing earth for what it thinks is the first time. The purity of the Fool is in the fact that he is unafraid of what will happen with his blind step because he does not judge but eagerly experiences whatever is meant for him to experience. He is excited about his journey. He is free of reputation and material accumulation and, therefore, has nothing to lose and everything to gain. See yourself like this in each new moment, and you will begin to let go of fear because you have let go of the idea that you have anything to protect.

Healing

There is no greater healing force in this universe than the combination of love and intention. We do not mean this is any metaphorical way. Your monks dedicate great amounts of time to the healing of the world through loving intention, not because it is a wholesome spiritual practice, which it is, but because it works. It really, really works. Your science is backing this up increasingly, so we need not work to convince you here but will go on to explain how you can apply it to your benefit and to the benefit of those you love.

Disease is born of disharmony. It begins with energetic disharmony that develops when, instead of using a negative emotion to steer away from or address something, you allow the bad feeling, and thus the problem it identifies, to remain and grow until it becomes a physical or situational manifestation. The antidote to this of course begins with committing to identify the source of the negative feeling and dealing with it, however big it has been allowed to become. This is often referred to as Shadow Work. So that is one component of this. The other, the love component, as mentioned, is an energetic power shot to every cell in your body. Feeling unconditional love or having unconditional love radiated towards you literally triggers your cells to move back into harmony and health, especially when combined with a specific intention. When a parent kisses their child's boo-boo better, it is not just a cute trick; it is a literal healing tool, and it works. Love aligns the body with the spirit and thus allows the pure well-being of spirit to course through it, drawing it ever closer to its true state.

If you have ever been moved to tears by a sunset or moving moment, you have zapped disease out of your body and brought yourself closer to your optimal health. A single moment of ecstatic love and appreciation can cure a cold. Now imagine what a daily practice or constant state of love can do. Love tells your nervous system that all is well and thus allows it to relax so that it may move from survival mode to general maintenance mode. Here your body relaxes. Here your body believes all is well and so becomes well. Here your mind eases into happy acceptance and all that plagued you becomes irrelevant, a distant dream. From this place of love you can now begin to look with more steadiness at the shadow aspects that manifested within you, seeing them for what they are without fear and judgment, appreciating what they have taught you, and letting go resistance against them, thus letting them pass through you with the easy assistance of your love.

From here you can take the action to change what in your life or your inner self your bad feelings have been pointing at, knowing that you want always to feel love and that nothing in your life is worth the suffering and disease it creates. No duty, no work, no friend or lover is ever worth your disease, and so have the courage to let it go. Have the courage to be happy and to be in love and you will heal yourself and in many ways those around you.

Affirmation for Healing

I am grateful for the manifestation of my unhappiness in physical form because it has brought to my attention that which I would not have otherwise addressed. I know that I can heal myself and others through the sheer force of my love and intention as well as through addressing that which caused the disease in the first place and by allowing myself to live only that which makes me feel good. I understand that the shadows in my life and those people and situations that seem to do me harm are within my control to learn from and move on from. I know that I am made stronger and wiser in each lesson and with each new glorious boundary and decision I make for my own good. I let resentment go and replace it with the wisdom that will allow me to eventually turn it to love and gratitude. I claim my power to rewrite my own story, knowing I am not bound to anything or anyone and that I can replace misfortune with well-being through the power of adjusted perspective. I am not defined by my past but by the present, which I have absolute sovereignty of. I take responsibility for the way I feel, accepting that it is no one's job but my own, and knowing that feeling good is what keeps me in good health because my good feeling means I am doing what's best for my body, mind, and spirit. I resolve to face each bad feeling as it arises, identifying its source and addressing it before it manifests or worsens. I know I am not supposed to feel bad and so never allow myself to stay in the bad feeling, not by forcing myself to enjoy something I don't enjoy, but by changing the thing itself or changing completely my perspective of the thing until it aligns with joy. I appreciate my hardships for what they have taught me and how they have strengthened my ability to heal myself through experience.

Boundaries and Letting Go

The setting of boundaries based on your own happiness has several effects that will likely shake up triggers and shadow elements that need tending. This is the beginning of your real work. As you begin to pay attention to your feelings and as you begin to care about them, knowing that they have the power and inevitably will either make you sick or vibrant, you develop new tastes and new standards for interaction. You begin to notice that the people you usually spend time with don't always make you feel good and begin to want to spend less time with them. You notice when someone is not authentic or when they take a jab at you and, instead of rolling your eyes or returning the jab, you want only to get away and find someone whose company is more pleasant.

This will happen with increasing degrees depending on how far down this path of self-realization you go, at the extreme leaving you in a space of isolation while you wait for your new tint of attraction to bring in the people who match it. This is a great opportunity for growth and refinement as it tests your ability to face criticism and attempts at manipulation by those who you are leaving behind, thus strengthening your tact and resolve, and as it forces you to learn to be alone and to wait and to have faith. Here the trick is not to regress based on loneliness or a desire to fit in again. You will only hurt yourself this way as your bad feelings will be worse than before and the disease resulting from discordant interaction will show up more strongly than before.

As you upgrade, your tolerance narrows. Notice that someone who eats a clean, raw, and sugarless diet will be made much sicker by eating a hamburger than one who eats nothing but hamburgers. This is a good thing. It is your new and improved self telling you it will not merely stand by while you slip back into that which doesn't serve you. Become patient and wise in this time. Know you are on your way to something greater and appreciate how far you have come. Sometimes this period of waiting after levelling up can be the most challenging phase of all because it asks you merely to sit in faith and keep up the joy without having any indication of what's coming next or where it's coming from. Know that something that is a match to you always comes. It is the law. Know that as you improve, what comes into your experience improves in equal measure. You attract what you are. Period.

As you heal and come into alignment with yourself, with all that is, letting it run through you with surrender and faith, your focus of concern shifts from self to other. You no longer need anything from anyone and the force of source energy, with all its well-being, urges you towards spreading that well-being to others. You wish to share your insights and you wish to hold others in a space of love and in judgment as they share whatever it is they want to share. You will notice people begin opening up to you more, wanting to be around you more, and generally feeling better around you more often. This is because you bring no discordant energy to the table and you make nothing about yourself, allowing them to make everything about themselves, which is fine, because you are here for them, not the other way around. The self-healed person becomes a healer of others in this way, emanating a healing love force and reducing the discordance in every interaction merely by being who they are and feeling how they feel.

Sit long with an empty mind and watch the world dance around you without trying to name anything or figure anything out and watch what magic occurs both within and "outside" of you.

Imagine walking into a room full of people having forgotten yourself entirely and being in a state of pure delight at getting to meet all the people you are going to meet. You are not worried about how you will come across because you are barely aware of yourself, and instead you stand in a state of abandon and appreciate and listen without worrying about a response, again because you are no longer in the equation. There is just the other person, just the presence of them and what it is they want to say and your eagerness to listen and to take them in. Imagine if someone approached you this way, how good this would feel. This is how you are making others feel and, interestingly, this is what makes you so pleasant to be around that you really needn't worry at all about how you come across.

Think of it this way: when you meet someone new, are you concerned about their accolades, their cleverness, or their strength, or how good they make you feel? If you have been practicing the principles in this book and are aligned with who you are, then the clear answer is the latter: how good they make you feel. See how easy and how fun every outing would be if you always felt this way and if others felt this way as well. Know that as you expect this and look for it in others, you increasingly find and manifest it in them. Do not judge or take note when they are not like this, just note when they are, in order to create more of it. Be curious and open and loving. Use every interaction as an opportunity to love, and you will make more difference in yourself and in this world than you will ever know. Use your phone call with your cable provider as a chance to love. Use your trip to the grocery store and your work in this way. Now everything becomes exciting because a simple task is transformed into an opportunity to literally heal both yourself and another. Notice what happens when you do this, see the relief in others when you treat them with love, the occasional delight, and let this inspire you to ever-increase this practice. Delight in what it brings and keep bringing more.

Affirmation

Each day I am seeing with more clarity and following my heart with increasing vigour. I am taking less personally and, as I look for the good in others, I notice that more good comes into my experience. I believe in well-being and believe that it is my birthright. I no longer linger in thoughts of my so-called failures but embrace thoughts of my successes, both now and to come, visualizing them with a clarity that lets me know they are manifesting. I love who I am and I love delighting in who I am becoming.

Like a cat finds the sunny spot in a room and stretches out there, find the emotional sweet spot in your surroundings and luxuriate in it. If you are in the middle of a triggering family dinner where there is debate and clutter, look for the happy dog in the corner, or the nicely decorated plate set. Rest your attention not on what you struggle with, though the go mind will think that is exactly wherein should rest its attention, as that will only increase the issue, but rather on the simple pleasure to be found in some visual or auditory element. If there is no such thing to be found — if you are in a war zone or being subjected to a torturous scene — find your breath and love the oxygen that comes in, love it consistently enough, and you will vibrate your way into more hospitable territory more quickly than you think. The longer you stay with the positive emotion, the more robustly material reality fills in around you in a way that reflects the good feeling.

Non-Physical

Understand that non-physical beings are not some magical notion, but are simply the points in consciousness that vibrate at a frequency beyond our three-dimensional spectrum of perception. This is where the distinctions of various dimensions come in. Know that your limitation in perception as humans is what makes your creative power so fun and so potent — it's what makes mystery and slow unfolding, as well as a wide spectrum of free will. Accept the reality of this and of the Law of Attraction. Accept that the way you feel is the key to self-healing and to manifestation and that your focus is your path forward. Accept that non-physical beings are pouring through you and your experience at all times in a steady stream of unwavering love and support. They are unlimited and ever-present, and they are ever waiting for you to believe in and call on them for assistance, for the law of free will dictates that they cannot interfere where not asked. How can you know that the higher dimensions are loving? It is easy: the frequency of higher dimensionality, after a point, vibrates at an octave of love — nothing can exist in that frequency that is not love-coherent. Being a non-loving entity in high-level dimensions would be like being a three-hundred-pound jockey. You just can't ride that horse.

Because they are not fixed to a singular point through the space/time/material reality we inhabit, they are capable of being multi-present. This is why ten thousand people can encounter archangel Michael in the same day. His consciousness and presence is not tied into the space/time continuum.

One of your goals here as a human on the Earth plane is to transcend limited and false beliefs and move up the spiral of awareness, seeing the illusion for what it is and learning to become lucid and intentional within it through the activation of love. It is not enough to become aware of the illusion and then remove yourself from it either through death or through isolation in an ashram or log cabin — in doing this you forget the second part of the equation, not just to wake up to the dream but to enjoy it, create it, elevate it through your lucidity. You are here to break out of the conditions but not the game. You are here to play the game as a master. You are here to inhabit and expand your glorious potential, to remember and regain your power, and to give the world the gift of your glorious awakened self. You are here to know that it is not so much about discovering your true self as it is clearing away false beliefs about your false self in order to make room for your pure being and to create from the clarity of that position.

The first thing you must fall in love with is your breath. All other love flows forth from the energy and self-relationship that exists in your love and cultivation of your own breathing.

Know that free will, to the degree that you experience it, is unique to the Earth experience and comes forth based on your agreeing to be ignorant to the true, loving state of reality in order to genuinely entertain the darkness that would help with your expansion. This is a lovingly-created playground. You came in as a relatively blank slate in order to encounter all the contrast and all the broad and versatile ingredients available only in a dimension such as this. You wanted to know and overcome and transmute pain. You wanted to know and find your way from confusion to clarity and from disharmony to harmony. It wasn't enough to just be in harmony. You wanted to grow through the internal efforts required to traverse such a terrain as this and so you set the difficulty level of your own experience according to what you wanted for your own growth. Think of this the next time you are tempted to say, "Why me?" And know that the answer is because it is your design and for your greatest good. Now what are you going to do about it. What are you going to make of it?

Collective Co-Creation

As you daydream, you create. As you dwell on the qualities and feelings of the world you want to see rather than the one you are seeing presently, you fill in the web of creation that makes it possible and increasingly probable. Now know as well that the more people actively engaged in this imagining and expectation of a better world, the more the web fills in and the more probably the reality becomes of materializing in your experience. So, keeping this in mind, we invite you to designate part of your day to sending loving intentions you would most like to see into the world. Imagine smiles and health and well-being, imagine it with love in your heart and know that millions of others are imagining the same things.

Be bold in your discovery of yourself. Be who you were as a child and embrace without judgment every single thing that makes you feel wonderful, not hesitating for a moment to send back anything that doesn't. Discard ideas about what you should or shouldn't be and discard the voices of others that move through your head with notions of the reality they believe to be true. Give yourself permission to get back into the space of thoughtless navigation by feeling. Give yourself permission not to know, not to categorize, not to strive, but simply to be. Accept the full spectrum of what pleases you without hesitation. Accept the full spectrum of your strength and your brilliance and your loving heart without reserve. Know that without a doubt the thing that makes your heart sing is the thing you came to do and every pursuit below this feeling is a divider and diluter of energy. As you become clear on this and, as we mentioned, you vibrate out of the vicinity of all that was, embrace your new spaciousness with the spirit of a pioneer and an adventurer, and allow the simplicity of all this clearing to sculpt you into the compassionate, easy, and happy person you were born to be. Listen through the quiet for the inner nudging of spirit and follow it without thought, knowing that, so long as it feels wonderful, the direction is good. Be easy about it. Have fun with it. Observe when you get into your flow state and begin creating easily and with a happy heart. Ease into it, milk it, enjoy it, but don't allow it to become too serious. It is your truth and your truth is easy and wonderful, it is not a job.

You are always simultaneously in flux and whole within the still point of creation. Peace comes as you relax into this paradox.

Know that life is not supposed to be just okay and it is certainly not supposed to be a struggle. It is supposed to be wonderful, easy, dynamic, and exciting.

Believe this. Give yourself this gift with the enthusiasm and undivided intent that a parent gives their child a birthday gift. Without resistance, take this idea for a test drive, even just for a few days, and see how it navigates, see what it uncovers and how it snowballs into proofs of itself. Believe your life force is love. Believe that this love never dies, but is only obscured by negative beliefs. Believe in your creative potential and in the potential to change the direction of your creations in any and every given moment.

Love

Whatever one thinks one is chasing, one is always chasing love because one is always seeking to return to one's absolute natural state and that state is love.

What's happened for so many is that love has become confused with the destructive and discordant states and behaviour that arise in people as a result of the seeking for love outside themselves: jealousy, need, betrayal, weakness, loss, disappointment, and so on. These are the outcomes, not of love, but of an attachment to others in the seeking of love that pales in comparison.

Do not seek love in others because love is perfect and human relationships by their very nature will and can never be perfect. Human relationships are designed to provide the contract that helps expansion. Perfection is in the singular still point of existence, in your consciousness, in rest, and in meditation. As soon as you add another point, you have polarity, contrast, expansion — not perfection.

This is not to say anything against relationships. These things are all a wonderful and integral part of the human experience and are fundamental to your growth. It is only to say that love cannot flourish here if one believes that here is where love is. Rather come to know love in yourself — know that it is always and inevitably there — and then radiate it outward from your abundance, sharing it with others rather than looking for it in them.

You needn't strive to attain or reach love within you for it is you. Instead, you only need to shed that which stands between you and it. Shed the ego mind that wants to make sense of everything. Let it know that it can't, and lovingly disallow it to waste your time any longer in this pursuit. Shed the fear of being hurt and know that the love within you cannot hurt you, just as your heart cannot hurt you; it can only be halted in its harmony by your own clogging of your arteries and so forth. This is a good parallel. Your heart, like love, is always working in your favour, tirelessly, and your mistreating of it is the only thing that slows it down. Exercise your love. Nourish your love. Avoid those substances, thoughts, and activities that hinder it, and like your heart it will serve you as long as you are alive.

Love is life force. Love is what is left when all else is stripped away. It is ever waiting for you to claim it, to feel it, and to spread it. It is well-being and when you let go of what holds you back from it, it pours through you with more potent healing than any drug ever conceived of. You manifested into your physical form through the sheer power of your loving intention and without love your intention would have fallen flat in the etheric realm of thought and will. It is emotion, when added to thought and will, that rallies the subatomic troops into formation and thus manifests on the material plane. It is through love that your parents kept you alive and through love that you continue to exist to this day. If the love in you were to fizzle out completely, so too would your last breath. Therefore, know that love is not an aspiration but a given, and your work in finding it is not to seek, but to let go of all that stops you from seeing that which has been staring you in the face since your birth with the big dumb smile of a happy baby.

Know that in every feeling of restlessness or discontent, boredom, or disease, you are experiencing varying degrees of being cut off from your true loving essence. Remember these feelings are your compass. They are saying, "Hey, you are love. Why are you so blind to it right now? Let's get back there, pronto." This should be so obvious, and yet for thousands of years humans have normalized negative emotion to the point that, to some, the idea of alleviating it by seeking that which feels better is seen as some kind of escapism or weakness. This is like holding your hand in a fire and, while it burns, saying to yourself, "Well, I could take my hand out of the fire, but wouldn't that just be running from my problems?" We say emphatically: no! The only real running away from your problems is sitting around in negative emotion refusing to identify its cause and failing to make appropriate adjustments to get back into what feels good. Because what feels good is always in the direction of what is true: well-being and love.

Meditation

Meditation is simply the intentional alignment with self through stillness. In meditation we come into relationship with our thoughts, teaching ourselves to watch, to allow without engaging, and to always bring ourselves back to the quiet, the stillness. When we achieve a suspended state of stillness in thought and body, we are in our truest form — beyond the illusion of time and space. Movement is in space and thought is in time. Without movement and thought one aligns entirely with their absence and thus touches the true beingness of potential, of love, and of unresisted presence.

Let's start with the basics before expecting you to achieve time/spacelessness. There are so many day-to-day benefits to this practice even when seemingly entirely unsuccessful. Do not put pressure or expectation on the process. Simply make yourself comfortable for twenty minutes in the morning and twenty minutes in the evening. Relax your body and let go of the need to move or adjust yourself. Relax your mind and let go of the need to tackle any issue that may arise. This is your twenty minutes of designated peace.

Once you are comfortable enough that you can be still, focus on your breath, taking slow, filling breaths, appreciating the grace of each one, noticing how it fills your lungs and moves so easily in and out, slowing with each exhalation until you are calm and focused. From here you merely want to maintain focus on your breath, seeing each thought at is arises, and as you see it, make the decision to let it go as you return repeatedly to breath. You may think twenty thoughts, you may think a hundred. It matters not, so long as you are continuing to be aware and to return your focus. In this way you are training yourself to have a conscious relationship with your thoughts rather than to be an unaware receiver of them. You begin to recognize that you have sovereignty over your mental landscape and as you practice this and begin to master this, you begin to master deliberate creation. You learn to steer through your thinking mind, letting go of thoughts that support what you do not wish to manifest and that make you feel bad, and moving towards those that do support your manifestation. Of course, thinking the thoughts of manifestation is a different process than meditation, but meditation is where you learn to steer. It is your training ground for conscious imaginative creation. From stillness comes creation. From clutter comes only more clutter.

On Stillness

Often as one begins the practice of meditation, one struggles to keep the body motionless. Inevitably an itch arises or some mild discomfort that sets you thinking that if you don't adjust now the discomfort will only get worse. Like learning to watch and not engage with your thoughts, learning not to react to physical discomfort is of monumental benefit. When your nose itches and you decide not to scratch it, not only are you showing yourself that an itch goes away on its own, which you will see it do the moment you return your focus to your breathing, but that in denying your impulse and desire to scratch you are developing your willpower in a valuable way. You learn here that there is power in stillness, that all things pass, and that, in your calm focus, the discomforts of the world, your mind, and your body are free to come and go without your engagement, without needing to be pushed against or drawn out. You begin to feel the awesome power in your own overcoming of small temptations, in your choice to be still. You see that what perhaps you thought was a big deal was merely a passing temptation. An itch in meditation is a very good example of something the ego creates in order to shake you from your stillness. Your ego mind in this way, as it tempts you with thoughts and discomforts and as it pleads with you to get anxious again and start moving, is really what they have been referring to for years when they refer to a devil or demon. Therefore, enjoy meditation as a hero enjoys slaying their dragon. Each time you overcome a thought or an impulse you win a battle, become stronger, and gain more ground within the terrain of your inner self. Once you have been in stillness and breathing deeply for several minutes, the energy in your body begins to flow without the disruptions so constantly otherwise created by your thoughts and physical movement. You feel this like a wind moving through you, a life force free to fill you up with the very well-being and good health you are made of. You begin to feel coherence in your brain and in your body as pathways synchronize like ships coming together after a storm, in harmony and ready to move as needed.

The more you practice meditation, the easier your life becomes. You find you can slip into a meditative state at will, relaxing into your breath and finding your personal calm as those around you scurry and complain. You find you can decide what you want to think about rather than being pulled around seemingly against your will. You fall asleep quickly and wake up invigorated. You lose the need to react, and gain a quiet curiosity as others speak. You become more aware of your surroundings, and your response time quickens as the clamber of thoughts no longer cloud your instincts. You become easier to be around, and find others easier to be around as well. You feel your body with more clarity and begin to eat and drink differently, to move differently. You have a deeper sense of your own power, as you practice control, and thus begin to see and understand how much of your life you actually shape. In this way your life begins to change. It can't not. It changes for the better.

Be patient in all things. There is no finish line and no rush to get to any given point. Instead be wholly present in each moment, aligned with your own happiness, and with the flow of all that surrounds and runs through you. Look others in the eye and find that place where you are so present and so clear of thought of yourself or of past and future that you completely and utterly care about them. You may not care entirely about what they have to say, because often what they have to say has its own confusion and incoherence, but you care about them, and you see the unity in them, you see that they are manifested from the same quantum field you are manifested from and you begin to see them as yourself.

On Children

You cannot spoil a child with too much love. Love children unabashedly and allow their love towards you and towards all things to flow with the same unresisted force. They come in as pure love and if you allow it to continue and create a receptive and reciprocal environment for it, it will grow into a force of tremendous power. Use your children as an opportunity to return to your own childhood innocence rather than to teach. Life will teach them, and, aside from a few physical basics like "don't touch the wood stove" and "this is how you put on pants," they really don't need you telling them how the world works. Just as we encourage you to replace dictum or various teachings with experiential observational wisdom, we say to allow children to do the same. They have the advantage of not having to undo any false ideas and are free to experience from scratch. Therefore, do not be the one who begins to plant ideas in their minds about the way reality works. It would be wiser to ask them than to tell them. Their capacity for experiential learning is genius level and so often, almost all the time, this capacity is squashed by the adults in their lives who insist on pressing their minds into predetermined systems of reality.

Sit with them in honest and frank dialogue. Help them see the effects of their actions, not by telling them, but by asking them to consider the experience from new angles. For instance, when a child insults another child, sit with them before bed and ask them if they remember the look on the other child's face after they were insulted. Ask them what they think that look meant. Ask them what it feels like to think about this, and so forth. It is so much more effective to get an understanding based on experience rather than telling them flat out that something is wrong or harmful. They need to know why it is wrong or harmful and they can only know through exploring their own perception of experience.

It is not uncommon for a child's spirit to be more evolved than its parents. In this case a parent can become subject to intense scrutiny as the child takes nothing for granted and doesn't hesitate to point out flaws in reason and action. It is best to be humble here and learn from them while providing a stable and loving sense of security at the same time. They may guide you in the evolution of your spirit as you protect and support them in their evolution in flesh. It is a supreme gift, though it asks a lot of you. Know that when a lot is being asked of you, it is because you have the opportunity to really bring yourself to new heights. It is always best to accept this call and allow the gifts to push you outside your comfort zone.

Don't be afraid to be magnificent. Don't be afraid to play with abandon, to look without bashfulness, to engage without hesitation. You did not come here to learn the rules and fit in as best you can. You did not come here to learn how not to make waves. You came to make waves, to express your authentic self, and to help others feel safe enough and comfortable enough to express theirs which you do simply by demonstration. You came to take chances and to experience wholly and beautifully all that you could. You came to be ecstatic and unapologetic as you sorted through what you didn't like and made piles of what you did, like a bird gathers thread for its nest.

Stages of a Spiritual Awakening

If you believe and put into practice long enough what we are sharing here, you will eventually find yourself in the midst of what many call a spiritual awakening. This means that, through the clarity of meditation and of following your feelings, you will have begun to see through the illusion of the matrix, the programming of the game. You understand that all is dream and see yourself for the spiritual being you are, inside a human experience you didn't realize until now was a mere game of dress up. There are many layers to this awakening and we can't in good faith describe it in accurate enough detail to suit everyone who reads this book as so much of it is individual and unsayable.

It begins with a divine discontent, meaning you reach a point in your life when you realize that all you have been chasing has not made you any happier, and you feel something just isn't right with you or with the world. This is a blessing of the deepest kind as it is what makes you desperate and curious enough to begin exploring alternative views of reality. From there you begin your search and inevitably end up at books like this one. Some rare and lucky folks get their information from solitude in nature, but few of us modern people have the option, and for us meditation and wisdom teaching is the open door though which we begin our journey. As you read or listen, you find a certain resonance with the content of these teachings, seeing the truth as you apply it to your own experience and, more importantly, your feeling reaction. You let go of stigma and of how you once identified yourself and begin to take a chance on these unfamiliar approaches to your reality. This is where you most likely are now, if you're reading this book with honest investment: the cracking open of the mind and the opening of the heart. There is an awakening through knowing, and there is an awakening through feeling. To really advance or ascend as we say, you must reach the awakening of feeling. Here, the heart energy centre clears and your love pours forth for likely the first time since you were a child. This is the ecstasy that makes saints, for this is the opening of the floodgates that allows energy to move from your lower survival centres to your higher spiritual centres. It is through the opening of the heart that you gain access to everything beyond the societies of man, and from there the journey only expands outward and upward without end.

There is no way to willfully induce a heart opening. It can't be sought after or thought into being. It is a monumental power that is always there and that is waiting for you to let go of what holds it back. Its freeing comes without warning and with a crippling intensity. Robin fell to her knees, then further placed her forehead to the floor in reverence to the overflow of gratitude she felt for all she had ever experienced and was experiencing, without exception. Her feeling of unconditional love was so great she thought she might explode into light and disappear into it. She cried the unrestrained cry of a baby, drooling and unable to open her eyes for the force of the tears, then, when she could stand again, she danced for hours in pure celebratory joy. The only words she could say were, "Thank you." The feeling came seemingly out of nowhere. She had not been meditating on love, nor had she been thinking about someone she felt love for. She was living alone and hadn't been in a loving relationship ever. She had little to no family and not a whole lot of reasons, on paper, to be grateful. The things that flashed through her mind, in fact, as she felt this gratitude included some of the things one might consider bad: abandonment, abuse, poverty, etc. See, in this state of pure unresisted love she could see the perfection in all she had experienced. She knew all was well and all was by design, not because she had read it but because she felt it. She knew it. We tell you this because we want you to understand that love is not conditional. The opening of the heart is not conditional except that it requires your surrender. How did Robin surrender? It was simple. She sat, without intention, in front of a window, and was so lost in the movement of the leaves that she forgot herself, and it was in the forgetting of herself that she found the ecstasy of truth. Now of course you may have sat at many windows and watched many leaves blowing in the wind without having this experience. There are many other factors at play and they will vary from person to person. Diet helps, meditation helps, clarity helps, prayer and a general spiritual practice helps. Do not worry about how or when it will come and do not try to make it happen. Simply know that if you practice what we have taught and meditate on a regular basis with the sincere intent to still your mind and be, you will set yourself up to experience this to one degree or another. This is the beginning of your moving from seeing the illusion, to feeling beyond the illusion.

Here, your life changes irrevocably. You cannot invest in the things you used to invest in because you can see the ways in which they fuel the illusion. You see your friends and family differently, noticing the ways in which they complain or remain fixed in the cycles you now know how to break. You will likely want to guide them out and will soon discover this is a lost cause that only serves to again sever the clear flow of your own energy. Therefore, upon awakening, learn to let others be. Become the observer and the example. Do not explain or reprimand, but let be and bring love to the interaction.

It is isolating to be in this space and you will be stronger for having taken it on and learned to be in it. Know that in time you will attract to you those people who are also awake, and you will once again be able to speak frankly about reality as you know it to be. Until then, hold fast and enjoy the development of your character as you learn patience, endurance, and acceptance. After the initial opening of the heart energy centre, which, by the way, leaves you feeling blissed out and drunk on life for a languorous amount of time, comes the inevitable inner work. Some like to call this the dark night of the soul; some call it Shadow Work. Robin simply thinks of it as the fine tuning that follows discovery. Here's how it works: as your heart opens the energy flow to the upper energy centres, the upper energy centres shine light on the imbalances remaining in the lower. They thus expose and draw out imbalances for clearing, and it is then your work to see, address, and integrate each imbalance as it arises. Many get lost in this phase, not knowing that it is a part of the process and merely seeing each imbalance with a sense of distress and self-judgement. If you have been practicing the Law of Attraction, and feeling good, you will be able to navigate this phase with relative ease, though we will not lie and say it is not work. It is work. It is just easier and even fun work if you can look at it in terms of positives, seeing each illumination as an opportunity to learn and improve rather than a chance to chastise or be upset with yourself. We will explain this with an example.

Robin's fine tuning involved, for instance, a period in which every day she was confronted by the same situation and every day she left off feeling she had failed herself in some way. She finally recognized that the situation she was failing herself in was repeating itself (like in the movie *Groundhog Day* or the series *Russian Doll*) so that she could identify the discordance within her that was allowing this to happen, and thus have the opportunity to practice getting into balance until she could create new outcomes. The situation arises until you learn to change it. No exceptions. The quicker you catch on to the nature of this game, the more quickly you can get yourself out of these unwanted loops. So it is not such a dark night of the soul when you see and understand it this way, rather it is a speeding up of the action in your video game so that you may master your character and clear the last of the monsters before levelling up. Once you clear these cycles, you enter a period of rest and integration. You begin to get your sea legs, so to speak, as the shock of your awakening, and the exhaustion caused by your fine tuning, eases up, and you relax a little, back into your everyday experience with a certain groundedness. This is on the ideal track. Of course, there are many forks in the road here and many detours. For some, ego gets hold of all that has been accomplished and you may run away with your new identity, gaining a sense of superiority and falling back into the trap of identification and falsification again. This is only a detour and just about everyone will experience it to some degree. It's only natural the ego should want to take ownership of such a shiny new thing. The trick here is always to get back to love — move into the heart and remember that you got here through humility and love, not through superiority and being right. It is that very humility and love that will get you back on track. From here there is integration and grounding as you accept the nature of reality, and you accept that you live in a reality that those around you cannot see.

You own this with a quiet wisdom and begin to find a way to live it, striking a balance between being true to yourself, and peacefully coexisting with the rest of society.

You will learn here that one of the keys to this integration is to talk less and listen more. You will find that talking about yourself inevitably leads to others being uncomfortable or confused, and so will find ways to keep the conversation on them. You will likely choose not to engage in too lengthy philosophical or personal conversations with those who are not ready to hear them. It is your work to read people now. It is your work to present love and peace, over cleverness and rightness. Do not ever expend any energy arguing and do not fall again into the trap of choosing sides. Remember your awakening is based in non-judgment and can only be cultivated and grown in the same spirit.

You will likely want to find new work, work that allows you to apply what you know to helping others and serving humanity in a deeper way than most jobs allow. You will learn to be patient and to let spirit and your feelings guide you towards that work, knowing you will be supported by spirit along the way. Each day is another opportunity to refine as you strike balance between your spiritual and material existence, and at this point — at all points — it is imperative that you maintain your meditation practice at all costs. Without this you will fall so quickly out of balance and into the confusion again of the illusion. Remind yourself daily that this is an illusion, that you are in control, and that all is a reflection of our inner landscape. Use everything as an opportunity to grow, and do not worry about others as you do so. Know beyond a doubt that your mere presence as an awakened person, especially a happy one, has more impact than you will ever know.

Another effect of a spiritual awakening is an increased communion with non-physical or the spirit world. You will find an increase in messages and synchronicities, and will find that the nudges away from what doesn't serve you or towards what does become louder and more aggressive. You may also find, if you have done a thorough job of fine tuning and thus karmic clearing, your karma begins to hit you instantaneously. For instance, if you give away your power or speak ill of someone, you may step on a pin within seconds and cry out in pain. This is because, having cleared your karma and thus freed yourself of the obligation to return to Earth for more lessons and clearing, any new negative karma you take on is balanced right away in order to keep your slate clear. This is also spirit's way of keeping you on course and letting you know when you've slipped off the aforementioned narrow path. Once you're on, kid, you're on, so make sure you're done exploring contrast and polarity before you take on this journey. For many, a spiritual awakening is akin to rehab — one only goes once one has hit rock bottom and can take no more. Whenever you feel weary or unsure of the path, just remind yourself of the state you were in during your divine discontent, your rock bottom, when you decided to take this on.

Many people experience their awakening with a guide, often in India or at a designated retreat. This can be helpful for navigating what can otherwise be a very overwhelming experience. However, it is important, when you go back into your life, that you learn to navigate your awakening in your own way, and that you maintain your practice with a personal discipline that was not required when you had the structure of a guide, guru, or retreat centre.

When in doubt, whatever the stage or situation you are in, the answer is always the same: return to your heart centre. Return to love. There is nothing this state can't change for the better. This is our absolute promise to you. The decision to move from mind to heart brings peace within and transforms outward situations in a way cleverness or intelligence, and certainly worry, never could. Your love — being in your love, becoming love — is your greatest power, and once you learn to find it authentically in any situation, you become one of the most powerful people in the world. This is what Fred Rogers learned and just look at the impact his presence and work has had on the world.

Romantic Relationships

Many relationships end as people begin these practices. The relationship they are in, like most of the circumstances in their life, is the result of an old and outdated, unconscious point of attraction. This is fine. Endings are natural and even good. It is a human construct that, once coupled, people should feel obliged to commit to one another in spite of growing apart internally. The purpose of relationships is not to be a lifetime union. It is not a support system, and it is not a means to fulfilment. It is simply a fast track to self-discovery and mastery, as close proximity to any other human inevitably applies the mirror effect, showing you more of yourself than you could ever discover in solitude. Therefore, accept your intimate relationships for what they are, a tool for expansion. Through them you see yourself and you see more of the world as you gain insights through your partner's perception and experience. It is massively beneficial. Think of everything you learn by being near someone else, opening your life to experiences and ways of being, meeting people, and going places you wouldn't have otherwise. And we do not mean to suggest this is all there is to a relationship. While its main function is education and expansion, it, of course, serves to enrich the day-to-day, to infuse your life with the health and well-being benefits of physical contact, cuddles, hugs, and sex. There is the creative act of child-bearing and of preparing and maintaining a home. There is the expansion of family connections, the welcoming of new energy into life, and children have children, and so forth. Enjoy all of this for what it is, knowing that it is always going to be in flux because everything is always in flux, and no single relationship will last forever, certainly never the way it began. Allow the change that comes with growth and rather replace expectation with appreciation. The people around you become what you perceive them as, so if you insist in focusing on your partner's shortcomings, guess what you will amplify in them: their shortcomings. Every time you notice the undone dishes, choose to move your focus instead to the patient receptivity to your conversation over the dinner table, the kind smile, the offer to pick up the carrots or take out the garbage. We don't ask you to become a pushover or a doormat, but to keep your mental energy fixed on what is going well in order to amplify it. If and when something needs to be addressed, in an enlightened relationship, it will be easy to do so because you will have cultivated an open and easy flow of communication. There will be no defensiveness or misunderstanding, just an eagerness to know where one another is coming from in order to reach a reasonable solution. Every conversation amongst well-adjusted, awakened humans goes this way because the ego is not given free range to run amok as it sees fit, feeling it is being attacked and thus needing to defend. Instead, the spirit stands in perfect love and receptivity, seeking only to better understand, from a position of compassion. A relationship between two awakened souls is one free of conflict. That is not to say they won't disagree; their disagreement will simply never end in unpleasant actions or angry words towards one another because it is the defensive ego and the defensive ego alone that ever seeks to put down another in order to keep itself feeling afloat. One who is in harmony with their spirit seeks only ever to soothe and bring joy to others because they know there is nothing but more suffering to be found in anything less.

It takes time to strike a balance between compassion for others and a healthy self-interest. One must relearn interaction and find the sweet spot in how one responds to and approaches others, especially when conflict presents itself or if one or other issue needs addressing. One of the keys here is discernment: identifying what is worth your energy and what is not. You may, for instance, feel compelled to engage in conversation with someone who speaks boldly against your principles, from a point of pride or even just the good intention of enlightening them. This is the kind of conversation that can quickly devolve into argument and that will always be an unnecessary drain on your energy. You gain nothing from arguing, and it is very unlikely they will gain anything either, even if the point you wish to make is a life-changing one. Anyone who approaches you in a manner of argument is not looking to discover so much as to disprove and so this makes them an unlikely candidate for change. Reserve your energy and your good nature by moving away from such confrontations, and instead focus on those issues that really do need your attention. When you do find something that requires your attention and is worth your energy, approach it with ease and compassion and watch it sort itself out, unravelling like perfectly spooled thread. People are so rarely approached in this manner that when you choose to do so, they are more often than not so pleased by the rarity of respect they are receiving that they are eager to hear you out and accommodate.

Think of everything you do, think, and say in terms of energy. Pay attention to the words and actions that most seem to drain you and those that nourish or replenish you. Pay attention to the way you feel in every interaction and ask yourself if it was worth it. Your energy is your creative power. The more preciously you protect and maintain it, the more potent you become. Those who make the biggest headway in life — your great leaders, inventors, and artists — made it to the seemingly superhuman level they did by learning about and cultivating their own energy. They did engage in debates with their uncles over the dinner table, but retired early to wander the grounds, listen to the birds, and then, in a wonderful and easy headspace, went back to the work they loved in order to work towards the manifestation of their dreams.

Characteristics of the New Human and How You Are Becoming It

When we refer to the "new human," we refer to the metamorphosis you are undergoing as you shed the illusions of the man-made world and reintroduce yourself to yourself through this releasing. As millions of people begin to align with who they really are, stepping out of the rat race and into the easy presence of a sunny day, we now fully enter the dawning of the Age of Aquarius. Sacrifice and struggle are no longer the fashion. Here is the time when, by the simple opening of hearts, the world comes into harmony, exploitation dwindles, and co-operation becomes the norm as those who are divorced from their true spirit-self become the minority and the majority, now increasingly aligned, begin to set the tone for the masses.

The new human is without motive, but, like a child, approaches each new interaction and object with wonder and discovery, knowing no two moments are quite the same and so never becoming dulled by a sense of repetition. The new human is in touch with intuition, and can read the energetic signature of others without thinking or seeing information, but by merely feeling and identifying the source of the feeling. They are ever fine tuning themselves so as to best serve the world they want to live in. They value kindness over intelligence, warmth over wit, and laughter over ceremony. They are spontaneous and easy to be around. They are not interested in material accumulation, though their lives are always filled with abundance and all their needs are always met. They see only health and well-being in others and so create more health and well-being in others through the energetic signature of their projection. It is not that they are blind or ignorant to ailment and misalignment, but that they see it is a mere shawl thrown overtop a perfect soul.

The new human, as you are becoming, have anchored the spirit into the body and cohabitates, so to speak, with their higher self, training the ego as one trains a wild horse to work for, not against them. They listen to their bodies and to the energies of the people and spaces around them, navigating with ease into always the calmest or loveliest seas both inward and out. They are disciplined but not rigid, energized but not erratic, peaceful but not pushovers. Like Saint Francis, they seek not so much to be understood as to understand, not to be comforted as to comfort. They are those that are strong enough and wise enough to hold space for others as they begin their journeys. They know they are eternal and so take nothing here all too seriously in the long view, and yet treat every moment with the eternal importance it truly has. They know that past and future are illusions, that the mind is a trickster, and that their lives are the result of their own creative power.

As new humans begin to take root in the world, they anchor more love than the world has so far known and thus inevitably shift the collective, making that love all the easier for others to find within themselves. They feel the holiness and awesome nature of the Earth and so treat her with respect and deep appreciation. They want only the best for others, and wholeheartedly celebrate each success. They hold a quiet, happy wisdom that does not seek to prove itself but simply is. They set others at peace, and create spaces all over the world where others may come and begin to relax into the truth of who they are without fear of judgment or ridicule.

The new human does not hustle or worry and does not create messy scenarios in the present or future because they have learned to control their thoughts and thus their reality. Collectively their self-control begins to reflect an increasingly harmonious environment as you will begin to see communities, towns, cities, provinces, and even countries take on increasingly altruistic and highly functional policies, policies which could only come from a new human with their love and their powerful abilities to manifest and thus create change. You see the road we are leading you down here? This isn't just about self-mastery for your own sake and for the sake of your well-being and abundance, though it is very genuinely that as well. This is about rallying the troops, so to speak, opening enough hearts, and refining enough personalities that we can begin to shift the trajectory of your entire planet towards one of harmony and well-being.

It was with the mass awakening that resulted from these lockdowns as well as from an overall shift in your atmosphere that this brighter future became possible, and we are pleased to say the probability of what you would call a return to Eden has increased beyond our wildest expectations. The universe is watching, Earth, and we are eager for your success. Never before has a planet so rooted in destiny and illusion awakened to this degree, shifting from the illusions of the three-dimensional reality into the higher vantage point of the soul self in the fifth and, for some, sixth dimensions. What this means for you both in material and spiritual terms moving forward is more fantastic than you can presently conceive based on the materials of your past experience. Be ready to step into unknown terrain. Get ready to feel joy and mystery and magic, to experience ease and manifestation at the level of a dream. You have been lost in the fog for thousands of years and, as you come into the light and begin to shed your layers, we stand by emphatically celebrating you at every turn. We adore you. We praise you. We are taking notes and recording your transition for the cosmic records. It is truly historic and has affected the totality of existence for the better. Each time, in fact, one of you moves towards your soul self, conditions improve for the whole of us — the macro and the micro is the same, and with each cell there is a ripple that touches solar systems. You are waking up to your god nature, and your trajectory is so inevitable now that we see the shackles of the modern world, with its excessive thought and structure, collapsing as a rusted tractor finally dissolving to dust in the storm of your love. You are beginning to listen to yourself. You are beginning to see through the seeming authority of those you used to trust. You are thinking for yourselves, are caring about how you feel, and just as much, how those around you feel. Your empathy is increasing and larger numbers of you are sitting in loving intention for the betterment of the world. There is more genuine prayer now, more meditation, and more unity consciousness, and you shed the ego desire for shallow fulfilment. We see you falling in love with more present moments. We see you wanting better for yourselves and for your world. We see your unwillingness to accept less than wonderful, and we see, as some of you for the first time recognize, the choices you have where you previously thought you had none. We see a new strength emerge, one based not in conquest but in holding space. We see patience where there was anxiety and we see appreciation where once there was only a sort of hurried overlooking of all the day-to-day miracles in front of and all around you. We surround you and watch at all times without judgment but with the desire ever to be called to help in any way we can. And when not called upon, we stand here radiating our love towards you, which is the most we can do to help without infringing on the oh-so-valuable free will which is integral to the nature of your mission here on Earth.

We see your light increase, we feel your love, and we happily watch the vibrant webs of creation you begin to create as you take heed of our teachings.

We have taught humanity before but never to such a glorious end, for you are finally ready to operate in a purity of intention ripe for enlightenment and ascension. It only gets better from here and, while we understand you may be looking at the present global situation and feeling that the opposite of what we say is true, we assure you that what you are seeing is the tower collapsing, making a big old ruckus as it does. It will flail a while longer but know without doubt that it is out, it can't sustain in a world with this many awake souls, with this much light, it is simply not possible within the frequency that is now increasingly coming into being.

Know this. Sit with this fact and feel the wonderfulness of it. The more you know this, the more you feel it, the more quickly it will become a reality in material evidence. Set your intentions on it and we promise you will see innovations, reforms, restructurings, inventions, and new leaders that will literally rock the energetic and material structure of all you have ever known. This is it, kids — this is your chance to participate, not only in your own advancement and awakening, but in an age of enlightenment that will go down in history as the greatest transformation, not just on your Earth, but in the whole of the cosmos.

Even if you find this hard to believe, let yourself believe it. Let it be your reality and see how differently you move about your day, and within your own mind. Let skepticism fall from you like dust. It serves no purpose but to add friction to your beautiful presence and your beautiful creations. Forget the idea of the smarty-pants who questions all and believes none. It is a tool of the spiritless, of those afraid to be wrong as if there can be any objective right or wrong. Remember this is a dream and you are a dreamer. Seek not a truth outside yourself but choose your own adventure, choose your own truth, and let it fill in the webs around you until it becomes as quantifiable a reality as your gravity.

Again, we ask you not to take our word for anything, but to ask yourself what would you rather do: respond until death to the information others present to you as seeming facts, or become an artist, creating a magical and loving future for yourself based on faith and enthusiasm? Are you a reactor or a creator? Are you prepared for mystery or too comfortable in the well- trodden to strive off and forge anew? It really is up to you, and we know many of you will remain with the ship as it goes down while the rest discover not only is the water warm, but you can breathe under water and swim down to a world of your own imagining. This is heaven being offered without your having to die. This is us emphatically inviting you to stop lingering at the gates and come in, leaving behind all that holds you back, and accepting a rebirth of the most profound and delightful kind. We ask you what, really, do you have to lose?

Meditations and Visualizations

Manifesting Abundance

Sit or lie down comfortably. Cover yourself with a blanket if you chill easily. Make sure you will not be interrupted for a while. Breathe in, feeling the warm loving air around you filling your lungs with white light and when you breathe out, breathe out love and ease. With each breath, feel your body and mind relaxing more and more until you can barely feel your physical presence, just the steady and nourishing passing of air in and out. Feel this with an underlying appreciation for the constancy of your own breath, for the life force of it and the way in which it connects you to all that is. Once you are completely relaxed, let your heart smile, and let well-being wash over you as you begin to feel the feelings of having everything you want. Feel yourself in your best life like it is happening right now. Without getting too specific yet, allow yourself to focus primarily on feelings: the ease of abundance, the spaciousness, and the sovereignty. Feel the exhilaration of your holidays, the smooth handling of your car, and the beauty and spaciousness of your home. Feel the easy generosity of having everything you want and room to share. Let yourself smile as you continue, and don't worry if you cry or laugh during this meditation for it often can produce these results. Once you really get the feeling of it and feel confident in your joy and focus, you may begin to fill in a few of the particulars. Don't think about how the abundance will come, but do think about the wonderful results of it: the renovation, the palm trees, and the big family reunion in the Alps. Think about the places you will live and the people you will meet. Think about the warm, comfortable clothing you will wear and the healthy food you will eat. Think about the gifts you can give and the difference you can make in your life and in the lives of others. Don't be afraid to think big. As we say, it is as easy to make a castle as a button. See yourself as an abundant person. See yourself as a magnet for abundance and feel in your body what it means to have all that you need and more. The more you feel this in your body, the more effective the practice.

Note: It takes seventeen seconds for a thought to become a manifestational probability. Just think what you accomplish when you do this mediation for twenty unresisted minutes.

Also note: Remember abundance is not the byproduct of your broken system and is not a shallow perusing, but is a sign of spiritual maturity and positive vibrational frequency. You will not be able to manifest any monetary well-being if you hold contradictory beliefs of any kind. So please, get rid of them. Remember too that your abundance does not deny someone else theirs. Abundance is not a pie, and anyone who tells you it is, is misinformed. The more you have, the more you are able to bolster others, likewise, into abundance. You must develop a healthy relationship with money before attracting it. You must see it for the vibrational being it is and attract it with love and appreciation, for it will not come to one who does not think highly of it. Would you?

Manifesting Love

Sit or lie down comfortably. Make sure you will not be interrupted for a while. Breathe in, feeling the warm loving air around you filling your lungs with white light and when you breathe out, breathe out love and ease. With each breath feel your body and mind relaxing more and more until you can barely feel your physical presence, just the steady and nourishing passing of air in and out. Feel this with an underlying appreciation for the constancy of your own breath, for the life force of it and the way in which it connects you to all that is. Now as your body relaxes, and your mind slows and you begin to have some sovereignty over your thoughts, begin to focus on the feeling of being held by someone who loves you. Feel the warmth of it, the ease, and the safety. Feel accepted and nourished and seen for who you truly are without judgment or expectation. Feel your own radiance as the object of a loved one's gaze. Feel the twinkle in your eye as you look back at them. Feel walking down the road holding hands, feel sitting on a bench, touching thoughts, and touching shoulders. Feel the emotions of waking up on Sunday morning relaxed and contented in one another's company. Be as specific as you want without letting any logistics bog you down. Focus on things that feel good. Fill your home with their essence, and fill your body with their touch. Imagine dancing in the aisles of the grocery store and running to catch a train together. Bring these thoughts into your life and offer yourself nothing but pleasant and easy feelings about them. Imagine a person who makes you feel comfortable and one to whom you can speak without reserve. Imagine you feel as safe now as you did when you were a baby, like nothing can harm you because this person is just so pure, so gentle, so kind, and yet so inspiring. Imagine the energy that comes with good love, and the encouragement to be your best self without any sense of pressure. Allow yourself to sink into the you that you are capable of becoming in the company of someone who gives you the space and the love to continue becoming. Let yourself smile. Let yourself expect this love and know that it is on the way.

Note: This is a particularly good meditation for when you are drifting off to sleep as it will easily slip into your dream cycle and perpetuate itself and its effect there.

Self-Healing

Sit or lie down comfortably. Make sure you will not be interrupted for a while. Breathe in, feeling the warm loving air around you filling your lungs with white light and when you breath out, breath out love and ease. With each breath feel your body and mind relaxing more and more until you can barely feel your physical presence, just the steady and nourishing passing of air in and out. Feel this with an underlying appreciation for the constancy of your own breath, for the life force of it and the way in which it connects you to all that is. Now with each in breath, see your cells filling up with bright white oxygen, and see them as healthy and whole and hydrated. Fill them with love and let them know you are aware of them, are working with them, and appreciate all that they do for you. With each out breath release the darkness of your discordant energy, offering it up to your spiritual team to dispose of as they see fit. Do this for several minutes, then bring your focus to the problem area, infusing it with targeting love and light. See it as healthy, see it as pain-free, and begin to feel yourself as you are in your healed state: excited, vital, well, and free of pain. Imagine pleasure where there is discomfort or pain. Imagine ease. Imagine repair and strength. Focus on each cell and nerve ending in the area, and see them grow and thrive as they feed on the light of your loving intention. Know that they have been dwindling in the absence of your attention, and now that you shift your focus to them, now that they know you care about the work they do, they are revitalized and ready to heal you from within. Rejoice with every inch of your body as you finally make contact. Rejoice as you see what wonderful work your cells are doing tirelessly on your behalf. Know that wellness is your birthright and know that you are capable, with this intention, of returning to the perfection of your spirit manifested in your body. The longer you can hold the feeling of well-being, the more effective the healing will be. It often helps to add a prayer at the end of your meditation, asking for the assistance of a higher power and knowing that your prayer will be answered.

Note: Much research has been done on the efficacy of mediation in curing everything from allergies and diabetes to blindness and tumours. Look it up for an added boost of confidence and efficacy in your meditation.

Clearing Your Energy and Cutting Your Cords

We collect energy from others throughout our day which can often cloud and muddy our own energetic signature and point of attraction. It is a good idea to do a quick energy clearing and cord cutting at the end of each day, and in particular at the end of any engagement that leaves you feeling drained or as though you have taken on someone else's energy.

Energy can be picked up from strangers passed on the street and even from people in the houses or apartments you pass by. It can be picked up from watching a show or reading the news as well as from social media, as any thought form and emotional charge that is not your own is capable of having an impact. "Cords" refer more specifically to the energetic connection you may have to those you interact with more intimately. Parents and children have strong cords, as do co-workers and friends. Imagine a cord of energy like an umbilical cord reaching from each of your energy centres in various levels of intensity, to each of theirs. These cords are like contracts; they keep you tied together and thus acting a bit like mirror neutrons, instantaneously affecting one another. A quick way to determine whom you have cords with is to ask yourself who pops into your mind more than once or twice a day. Make this person or these people the subject of your cord cutting ritual as outlined below.

Sit or lie down comfortably. Make sure you will not be interrupted for a while. Breathe in, feeling the warm loving air around you filling your lungs with white light and when you breathe out, breath out love and ease. With each breath feel your body and mind relaxing more and more until you can barely feel your physical presence, just the steady and nourishing passing of air in and out. Feel this with an underlying appreciation for the constancy of your own breath, for the life force of it and the way in which it connects you to all that is. Ask the creator for a protective shield of white light and request that nothing that is not for your highest good enter into your space or awareness. Now call on your angelic team and your guides to surround you and ask that they clear your auric field. See them vacuuming the space around and through your etheric body, sucking out foggy and dense energy and leaving a polished, clear, and colourful aura. You will feel a lightening and a lovely clarity as this happens. You may also ask them at this time to rejuvenate your energy centres and then proceed to see them scooping out any discordant energy that may be blocking each energy centre from root to crown, sourcing it up with new colour and radiance as they go. Next call on Archangel Michael and see him standing before you with a radiant golden sword. See past him the person with whom you feel connected to through cords and ask that Michael sever the cords with his sword. Feel the relief as you see each cord fall and wither into the ether from each energy centre it was tied to. Feel the relief and the refreshing sense of renewal that follows this ritual. Stretch slowly as you come out of your meditation, and drink a glass of water to nourish the clear, radiant you that emerges now.

I recommend doing this every evening as well as upon returning from any intense social interactions.

World Healing and Collective Elevation

Once you become comfortable with meditation and feel you can hold your focus for an extended period of time, you may want to begin doing work for the collective. Your loving intent set on the well-being of the world has a substantial impact and so, once you are able, we encourage you to add your power to the many thousands who are already participating in this practice, and are helping to elevate the resonance of this Earth plane.

Once you are in deep meditation, see yourself sitting before a holographic Earth. You may notice that around the Earth is a ring of light beings, glowing gold and white and pink and emanating a welcoming presence as you sync your energy with theirs. Sit and unify with this ring, knowing that this is the collective of dedicated souls who take time out of their lives to sit in loving intent to heal the world. From here, breathe a little deeply, relax a little more, fall into your heart and, like a Care Bear, feel a wave of pure love coming out from your heart energy centre and wrapping the planet in a warm loving hug. Hold this feeling of love for as long as you can, focusing it on the Earth and all that dwells upon and within it. See first the people relaxing in your loving and energetic hug, then all the animals. See the waters clearing and the trees breathing. See the heartbeat of nature restored and the skies cleared. Practice maintaining this love, an unwavering compassion that sees not what needs to be fixed and fights not against what is discordant, but radiates purely and with an undisrupted wonderful feeling. Remember the world doesn't need your critique to help it heal. It needs only your love. When you are finished, bow to your collaborators and pray for an increased angelic presence upon the Earth plane as well as any healing and light that free will may allow.

Note: If you have friends who have read this book and who have been practicing these techniques, gather together to do world healing, and you will increase the potency of the practice.

Note: Remember that all healing depends on your seeing exclusively wellbeing. Do not see or consider the illness and injustice — just see the harmony and wonder that is and that is coming into being.

Practices

The Violet Flame

The violet flame is a powerful healing tool. It can be sent to someone without impeding their free will, along with loving intention, and is highly effective at relieving physical, emotional, and mental unrest. It is monitored by Saint Germain and so it is best to call upon Saint Germain before using it, asking in prayer and meditation for permission.

Once you feel you are a self-master — meaning you have cleared most of your karma, can watch and control your thoughts, and are operating from a place of loving intention and harmlessness throughout your life — you are likely a candidate for the use of the violet flame. You may use it on yourself, on another, or on the holographic world while in meditation. Simply see a bright cool violet flame rising up and consuming a holographic replica of the subject. Let it purge all suffering and confusion as it purifies and cleanses. It is always good to allow it extra time around the head as it is in the thoughts that most discordance originates and gestates.

When using it on yourself you will feel a wafting through your being, a slightly cool cleansing sensation. It is very refreshing and will literally restore health on all levels. Once you become good at using this, you will be able to heal people throughout your day with little effort. When I first mastered it, I tested it out by going to protests and demonstrations, using it where there was conflict only to see the conflict dissipate as the flame enveloped those involved. I will also note that, as I use the flame, I see the holographic replicas of those I'm using it on sitting in front of me in my pyramid of light. It is always their higher self before me, and they are always smiling the peaceful smile of one who knows what a blessing they are receiving — even if the physical version of them is yelling or crying. It is a wonderful reminder of our inner being's true state at all times.

I also like to use this method on anyone I may be struggling in life — taking them into my pyramid and making this offering so that I may see their loving inner being and help heal any discordance between us on this energetic level.

When using the violet flame or when healing others in general always ask for the best possible outcome and highest good for all involved. Many people do not — at the level of their inner being — want to be healed, as their illness is part of their soul's evolution. In these cases, which are many, your violet flame will serve to bring much-needed peace and relief as they experience what they must experience. Do this when you see an accident on the street or when you hear about a natural disaster or war on the news. This will help you remember that you are not powerless and will give you something more productive to do than feel bad or worried.

Note: It is always nice to finish off your violet flame practice with a waft of rose-hued loving intention — another sort of Care Bear heart burst to seal the deal and make everyone involved feel, at least on some level, wonderful.

Elevated Awareness

Sit on a bench in a park where you have a clear view of people and a large chunk of sky and field. Breathe deeply, relax. Let go of your thoughts. Watch the movement of human bodies without judgment or assessment. Don't notice how attractive or unattractive, or how poor or wealthy. Don't notice distress or happiness. Just observe. Observe until you begin to see the pure beingness of everything within your field of perception, until the trees and bees and dogs and humans and even the arc of the sky become the same thing, and until you become that same thing as well, inseparable. See the heavenly cords that come down as perfect and see how perfectly they drive the life force of every living being, and see how the seeming qualities of each of these beings is only a brief and fleeting mask of confusion. See that everyone is made of love. See that everything is made of love. See that all that is not is merely an illusion and a briefly-lived one at that. See how easy it is to love without reserve when you know this, when you feel it. See the comedy of it all, the players all on stage having forgotten that they are indeed playing a part, and do not hold it against them that they have forgotten. You have forgotten as well. It is our intention to forget. Only love them and know that you are no better for seeing this, only blessed with an opportunity to grow.

Get into this state whenever you feel bogged down in three-dimensional reality, or whenever you begin to forget you are in an avatar and start taking the play too seriously. Step back from your field of consciousness and see the divine underlying essence of all that is within each player — laughing at the madness of each role as it is acted out. Laugh too, inwardly. When others are seemingly running around as if their heads have been cut off, laugh inwardly with the love of a mother who sees her child crying over a spilled ice cream, knowing full well another even bigger scoop is on the way. Laugh, knowing all is well and all is as it is supposed to be. Laugh, seeing the love and knowing the lifetime is a sliver in the eternal expansion of all that is you and all that is everyone and everything you encounter. Laugh with the compassion of one who holds nothing against anyone but knows to their core the oneness, the singular energy, that we are woven from and to which we will all unravel again towards our own perfection. Look in the mirror and see the creator. Look at a stool and see the creator. Look at a man yelling at you on the road and see the creator/source energy.

~

Once you begin to really live in the fifth-dimensional reality, seeing with Unity Consciousness, communing with spirit, and operating with mastery of the Law of Attraction, it is important to adjust the way you communicate with others. This way of being is a direct line to the nature of reality, and, for many, direct experience of spirit is a frightening, even heretic, way of being. Many prefer having an intermediary work between them and all that is. Of course, we are emphatically calling you away from such intermediaries, but we are also imploring you to be very careful about attempting to call others away from them. We wrote a book so that those who were ready could come to us and find it. We do not jump into the consciousness of random people and work to wake them up against their free will and neither should you. Be extremely discerning about whom you share your knowing and experience with. Get used to being a bit mysterious as you keep those thoughts and experiences to yourself that are of a metaphysical nature. You do not owe anyone an explanation of your way of being or your beliefs and, more importantly, no one owes you their understanding or transformation. Do not judge or look down on those who remain rooted in materiality. This lifetime is but a small blip in their evolution and by just being within your presence, you have helped expedite that evolution profoundly. Therefore, stay quiet. Lay low, and let your love do all the talking. Learn to listen more than you speak, and watch how others begin to speak with more compassion and introspection in your presence, seemingly unprompted. Be patient and smile, knowing that your smiling has a healing effect your words never could.

Triggers

Inevitably, as you move along this path of healing and self-actualization, you will encounter triggers which will shake up the peace you thought you so securely had figured out.

Most often these triggers come in the form of parents; sometimes they take the form of a social archetype. It is important first to forgive yourself for being thrown off balance. It happens to the best of us. Next, work to return to centre through breath, take some space, and begin to unpack what it is that is left unhealed in you that allows this trigger. Of course, people can be awful in their behaviour, but if you had no buttons left, they simply could not press any. Therefore, a trigger indicates a button, and your aim here is to be button free. Sit in meditation, when you are well away and recovered from the trigger, and ask yourself what this person is mirroring to you.

Remember, no one owes you anything. No one needs to be or do or say anything for you and there is nothing wrong with anything anyone is doing or saying or being. Change what you can change: yourself, and watch the world fall into beautiful formation around your new point of attraction.

My Story

For years, I told the story about how my father thought I was a witch and so taught me magical spells, moon rituals, and astral projection. I told this story from the point of view of a sort of victim whose gifts were exploited by a father who would soon abandon her. I even wrote a book about it. My father died of lung cancer two years ago, and since then my relationship with him has changed, along with my perception of just about everything in my experience from birth to now.

My real awakening happened during lockdown. I had had glimpses of the divine before, massive moments or even days of ecstasy, and a certain knowing that there was something of great meaning and depth going on beneath the layers of day-to-day distractions. These were often short-lived. With no knowledge or teacher to build on, I just went from profound experience back into mundane life within weeks, feeling invigorated and healed on many levels, but not awakened. Some part of me knew that when the virus took off and lockdown became imminent, I would embrace the opportunity to shut out the world and go inward. That's exactly what I did. I created an automatic reply for my business that said simply "gone fishing," turned off my phone, and shut out all of my friends and family. I knew I needed to sever myself from outside influence in order to find out who I was when I wasn't adjusting for others or cluttering my own inner landscape with their words and vibrations. I soon discovered Abraham Hicks, who went just as viral as COVID-19, and as soon as I heard these teachings, it was as if a light was cast on my whole life story, showing it for what it really was: meaningful, created, adventurous, and mine. I took Abraham Hicks's advice and began focusing exclusively on positives while taking time to daydream about the things I wanted from life. At the time (just six months ago as I write this) I was living in a one-bedroom apartment in a dense area of Toronto. Next door was a halfway house for women who were in recovery from hard drug addiction, and on the other side of them was a building under loud construction. It was winter. It was dark. I was living off the canned lentils I had managed to store before lockdown went into effect. I knew that if I could focus on positives and find bliss in these circumstances, everything else would feel easy. I remember lying down for hours listening to serotonin-releasing frequencies in my headphones to drown out the jackhammers. I remember making playlists of songs that inspired feelings of magic and empowerment. I remember loving the feeling of my body sinking into the bed at night, feeling so grateful to be living alone and to be able to embrace at last the quiet that came with sundown. I remember falling in love with each and every plant in my apartment on a new level as they in turn sprouted new, pale-green baby leaves and flourished under the heightened vibration of my bliss. I swam in the clarity of my mind, void of thought, and relished each little activity throughout my day. Cleaning became a joy. Moving from the kitchen to the living room became a joy. Stepping outside during rare breaks in the clouds to feel the sun on my face was beyond joy — it was miraculous. I began to imagine with a feeling of deep appreciation and knowing, the house I wanted to live in. I focused on the feeling of it and what would bring that feeling: spaciousness, quiet, brightness, friendly spread out neighbours, families, unique style, apple trees, local food, community, privacy, room to grow, the ocean, the sky, ownership, and independence.

I realized as I followed the teachings of Abraham Hicks, though which I learned about LOA, that teachings are a bit of a trick. They are not just trying to get us into better homes and bigger bank accounts; they are moving us towards our own awakening. It's impossible not to begin to awaken as you focus your thoughts and energy on what feels good. It is an inevitable outcome. So within about two months I found myself breaking the veil, living a coexistence with spirit many would not believe if I told them. And now, just half a year later, I have manifested the perfect house, apple trees and all, and am sitting in my spacious sunroom as I write this. I am steps to the ocean on the greatest tide in the world, and am surrounded by kind, artistic people who are eager to make me feel welcome. I have everything I need and, since settling in, have been prompted by spirit to write this very book, knowing full well that it is the beginning stage of a new series of intentional manifestations on my part.

The experiences I have had over the past six months have turned the floodlights on my life and the lives of those around me, switching the narrative so drastically that I still must adjust my responses in conversation as I no longer can use any of the same qualifiers or narratives to describe who I am and where I come from.

The victim role that I for so long cast myself in has completely dissolved, and in its dissolving, I recognized and inwardly attuned for the harm I did to myself and my perceived victimizers every time I reinforced these narratives. I see now only teachers and opportunities to grow and strengthen. I now see the "witch" I thought I was as the spiritual being who came into this Earth connected and wondrous and full of synchronicities. I see the love I always had for my father and the strength I gained in our earthly drama together, and now that he is in the realm of non-physical, I know him without the distortions and confusion of his material self. I know him as perfect and I feel his presence ever assisting me towards more refinement, more love, and more joy. I forgive myself for the harm I caused when I didn't think or know about the effects of my words and actions, and have adjusted my behaviour accordingly since becoming aware. I see us as ancient friends in the astral realm, having agreed to come down in this lifetime and play these roles for another's evolutionary benefit. I see the comedy of it and the fun, and I see the wonder in the progress I have made, having woken up to forgiveness and joy after what would seem on paper a particularly negative starting place. I know that this negativity, or as Abraham Hicks calls it, contrast, has caused me to imagine and begin to manifest monumental new realities, and I sit here at this desk on the precipice of all that I know I am about to create from my newfound empowerment. I am sharing this with you because I want you to know what depths this clarity can be found from, and that sometimes the more severe the depths, the more spectacular the upswing — often actually. Jung famously says that for a tree to go up to heaven, its roots must reach down to hell. In this way, understand that all the misfortune and seeming disadvantage you have experienced is both a reflection of the power you have (you program your level of difficulty based on your capacity) and an opportunity to reach your roots down so low that you can reach glorious heights. The reward is a reflection of the work required, and the more work you have to do, the more deeply and brilliantly you will feel the relief and wonder of each reward as you move yourself up the spiral of enlightenment and ascension.

I am looking forward to the unfolding of my life as I am looking forward to whatever unfolds in yours as a result of the inner work you are doing. I can tell you from experience we are loved and supported so deeply by higher dimensional beings, and when we relax into this without fear and begin to take their guidance, we become masters. The game goes from tedious to fun, and the scenery improves by leaps and bounds.

This being said, do not get too caught up in the guidance of others in this realm, like mediums and psychics, as is often the temptation when you realize this is all quite real. The trouble here is you are vulnerable to the biased reading of the medium or psychic reader, and are also cutting yourself off from the cultivation of your own communication style with the non-physical. It is a tempting fast track, but can often lead to confusion and sometimes let down or even fear. Instead of trying to figure it all out, sit back and enjoy, knowing that it is there and is always working behind the scenes for your benefit. Even when things seem to be going wrong, they are always actually going right — just in more complex ways than you can see from your vantage point.

~

I want to talk more about the manifestation of the house, just to give a better sense of how this all works and to drum up your excitement a little. I manifested through imagining, through feeling, through focusing for weeks on end on the singular goal. When it came to material action, I began searching for houses that were in my budget and checked off most of my boxes. For months I made calls to agents for houses in New Brunswick and PEI, and for months I was turned away as one after another were already sold or had multiple over asking bids on them. COVID-19 meant that people like me could work from home, and so I wasn't the only one with the idea of escaping to the ocean. Instead of being discouraged with each rejection, I merely told myself that none of these were my perfect house, and that I was being continuously kept on track towards the ideal. Seeing the world and all its events this way makes a real difference in your mood and sense of reality. Suddenly all that once would have hurt or depressed or angered me became a blessing, and I went back to happily imagining and anticipating what I knew without a doubt was headed my way. I even began to see each rejection as further confirmation of my being guided as I knew deep down none of them was THE house. So, about three months or so into the search I remember having this listing for a big, red house in Nova Scotia up for days on one of the tabs on my computer. I hadn't been really looking in Nova Scotia, and I somehow felt like this one was too good to be true and surely wouldn't be on the market any longer (my ego stepping in with thought to sabotage my faith), but finally I gave the agent a call. She informed me that an offer had just been made and that there was a 9 a.m. deadline. We could put in our own offer in the morning if I felt brave and sure enough to buy a house sight unseen. I told her I would get back to her in a few hours and took those hours to check in with my guides. How do I do that? I meditate and I observe. In my observing I encountered signs of immense encouragement: repeating numbers, children walking by saying things like "It's perfect!" and "Go for it!" and a post on Instagram that said, "When you know it's yours sometimes you have to fight for it and move fast." I called the agent back and told her we would go in way over asking to make sure we got it — right to the tip of my budget. Our offer was accepted the next morning and I never once felt like I had been hasty because by that point I had learned to trust the language of the universe beyond a doubt. My guides see what I don't and know, better than any of my puny reasoning, what will make my heart sing. Now it gets better. I knew from the pictures that the house was large and unique and would give me the sunroom and dance studio I'd always wanted. I knew from word of mouth that the community was wholesome and artistic and welcoming. I knew little else. I began to daydream more, imagining what I would build and plant once there. I had a great aunt who kept apple trees and who would serve us fresh applesauce made from their apples. That had stuck with me and I'd always wanted to do the same. So I would plant apple trees. I would also build a raised garden and grow my own food in spring. And of course I wanted berry bushes all over the place. I also noted that the one thing I would miss when I left Toronto would be easy access to massage parlours. I love massages, but thought there's a very slim likelihood there will be any in the rural community of Kingsport. A few weeks before I left, I met with an old friend to walk through the U of T campus in Toronto. He pointed out with wonder a *Ginkgo biloba* tree on the path and I was completely taken by the bright simple fanning leaves and the overall grace of the tree. I fell upon it and hugged it with an overflow of love. It was one of the most special trees I'd ever seen and I knew about the healing properties of *Ginkgo biloba*. I didn't think much more about the tree. So, what I have discovered since moving here is that my property has on it: five apple trees, one blackberry bush, one blueberry bush, a raised garden ready to be planted, and a stunning, totally-not-local-to-here *Ginkgo biloba* which peeks out over the edge of the property, the first tree you see — a wedding gift to the previous owners fifteen years ago. On top of that the two businesses in town are the farm across the street that delivers the best produce I have ever had — all organic — and a world-renowned osteopath who also offers Swedish massage, less than a block from my front door. This is the specificity with which your manifestations occur, and the only way you can cut yourself off from its perfection is to jump off at the wrong point or stop believing and start overusing your brain. The moment you force something because you think it's right is the moment you cut yourself off from what the universe is over there gift-wrapping for you. It doesn't stop there, of course. Since moving in, everything I want for my home has shown up: from a perfect sofa and chair set the neighbours just happened to be looking to get rid of, to a display of pumpkins just dropped at my door in time for autumn. I look at a rocking chair I want online and find the same one on the curb within two days. It is gift after gift, and all that's required of me is that I keep believing, keep anticipating, and keep being grateful.

I could list another thousand jaw-dropping synchronicities but I imagine that would become a little tedious. What I offer here is meant to whet your palette, to get you believing and expecting the same, or even more, for yourself. Remember your expectation is a big part of this, a crucial part, and so believe what I tell you, let the wonder of it sink in. Now sit back and start putting all this into practice, and then watch your life begin to take on the form of a fairy tale.

~

We would like to end with a simple and beautiful story which serves as a helpful guide to everything you need to know about what it takes to be a good person here on this Earth plane and beyond.

Thank you for spending your time with us. We are excited about the unfolding of each and every one of your beautiful lives.

Fairy Gifts

from The Green Fairy Book by Andrew Lang

It generally happens that people's surroundings reflect more or less accurately their minds and dispositions, so perhaps that is why the Flower Fairy lived in a lovely palace with the most delightful garden you can imagine, full of flowers, and trees, and fountains, and fish ponds, and everything nice. For the Fairy herself was so kind and charming that everybody loved her, and all the young princes and princesses who formed her court were as happy as the day was long, simply because they were near her. They came to her when they were quite tiny, and never left her until they were grown up and had to go away into the great world; and when that time came, she gave to each whatever gift was asked of her. But it is chiefly of the Princess Sylvia that you are going to hear now. The Fairy loved her with all her heart, for she was at once original and gentle, and she had nearly reached the age at which the gift was generally bestowed. However, the Fairy had a great wish to know how the other princesses who had grown up and left her were prospering, and so before the time came for Sylvia to go herself, the Fairy resolved to send Sylvia to some of them. So one day her chariot, drawn by butterflies, was made ready, and the Fairy said, "Sylvia, I am going to send you to the court of Iris. She will receive you with pleasure for my sake as well as for your own. In two months, you may come back to me again, and I shall expect you to tell me what you think of her."

Sylvia was very unwilling to go away, but as the Fairy wished it, she said nothing. When the two months were over, she stepped joyfully into the butterfly chariot, and could not get back quickly enough to the Flower Fairy, who, for her part, was equally delighted to see her again.

"Now, child," said she, "tell me what impression you have received."

"You sent me, madam," answered Sylvia, "to the court of Iris, on whom you had bestowed the gift of beauty. She never tells anyone, however, that it was your gift, though she often speaks of your kindness in general. It seemed to me that her loveliness, which fairly dazzled me at first, had absolutely deprived her of the use of any of her other gifts or graces. In allowing herself to be seen, she appeared to think that she was doing all that could possibly be required of her. But, unfortunately, while I was still with her, she became seriously ill, and though she presently recovered, her beauty is entirely gone, so that she hates the very sight of herself and is in despair. She entreated me to tell you what had happened, and to beg you, in pity, to give her beauty back to her. And, indeed, she does need it terribly, for all the things in her that were tolerable, and even agreeable, when she was so pretty seem quite different now she is ugly, and it is so long since she thought of using her mind or her natural cleverness that I really don't think she has any left now. She is quite aware of all this herself, so you may imagine how unhappy she is, and how earnestly she begs for your aid."

"You have told me what I wanted to know," cried the Fairy. "But, alas! I cannot help her; my gift can be given but once."

Some time passed in all the usual delights of the Flower

Fairy's palace, and then she sent for Sylvia again, and told her she was to stay for a little while with the Princess Daphne. Accordingly, the butterflies whisked her off, and set her down in quite a strange kingdom. She had only been there a short time when a wandering butterfly brought a message from her to the Fairy, begging that she might be sent for as soon as possible, and before very long she was allowed to return.

"Ah! Madam," cried she, "what a place you sent me to that time!"

"Why, what was the matter?" asked the Fairy. "Daphne was one of the princesses who asked for the gift of eloquence, if I remember rightly."

"And very ill the gift of eloquence becomes a woman," replied Sylvia, with an air of conviction. "It is true that she speaks well, and her expressions are well chosen, but then she never leaves off talking, and though at first one may be amused, one ends by being wearied to death. Above all things she loves any assembly for settling the affairs of her kingdom, for on those occasions she can talk and talk without fear of interruption; but, even then, the moment it is over, she is ready to begin again about anything or nothing, as the case may be. Oh! How glad I was to come away I cannot tell you."

The Fairy smiled at Sylvia's unfeigned disgust at her latest experience, but after allowing her a little time to recover, she sent her to the court of the Princess Cynthia, where she left her for three months. At the end of that time Sylvia came back to her with all the joy and contentment that one feels at being once more beside a dear friend. The Fairy, as usual, was anxious to hear what she thought of Cynthia, who had always been amiable, and to whom she had given the gift of pleasing.

"I thought at first," said Sylvia, "that she must be the happiest princess in the world; she had a thousand lovers who vied with one another in their efforts to please and gratify her.

Indeed, I had nearly decided that I would ask for a similar gift."

"Have you altered your mind, then?" interrupted the Fairy.

"Yes, indeed, madam," replied Sylvia, "and I will tell you why. The longer I stayed, the more I saw that Cynthia was not really happy. In her desire to please everyone she ceased to be sincere, and degenerated into a mere coquette. Even her lovers felt that the charms and fascinations which were exercised upon all who approached her without distinction were valueless, so that in the end they ceased to care for them, and went away disdainfully."

"I am pleased with you, child," said the Fairy. "Enjoy yourself here for a while and presently you shall go to Phyllida."

Sylvia was glad to have leisure to think, for she could not make up her mind at all what she should ask for herself, and the time was drawing very near. However, before very long the Fairy sent her to Phyllida, and waited for her report with unabated interest.

"I reached her court safely," said Sylvia, "and she received me with much kindness, and immediately began to exercise upon me that brilliant wit that you had bestowed upon her. I confess that I was fascinated by it, and for a week thought that nothing could be more desirable; the time passed like magic, so great was the charm of her society. But I ended by ceasing to covet that gift more than any of the others I have seen, for, like the gift of pleasing, it cannot really give satisfaction. By degrees I wearied of what had so delighted me at first, especially as I perceived more and more plainly that it is impossible to be constantly smart and amusing without being frequently ill-natured, and too apt to turn all things, even the most serious, into mere occasions for a brilliant jest."

In her heart, the Fairy agreed with Sylvia's conclusions, and felt pleased with herself for having brought her up so well.

But now the time was come for Sylvia to receive her gift, and all her companions were assembled; the Fairy stood in the midst and in the usual manner asked what she would take with her into the great world.

Sylvia paused for a moment, and then answered: "A quiet spirit." And the Fairy granted her request.

This lovely gift makes life a constant happiness to its possessor, and to all who are brought into contact with her. She has all the beauty of gentleness and contentment in her sweet face; and if at times it seems less lovely through some chance grief or disquietude, the hardest thing that one ever hears said is: "Sylvia's dear face is pale today. It grieves one to see her so."

And when, on the contrary, she is gay and joyful, the sunshine of her presence rejoices all who have the happiness of being near her.